FOWL KNITS

By the same author
BEASTLY KNITS

FOWL KNITS

LALLA WARD

TECHNICAL ADVICE BY
BARBARA AND HELEN CLARKSON

SIDGWICK & JACKSON
LONDON

To the
Royal Society for the
Protection of Birds

First published in Great Britain in 1987 by
Sidgwick & Jackson Limited
1 Tavistock Chambers, Bloomsbury Way
London WC1A 2SG

Photography by Colin Thomas
Design by Laurence Bradbury
and Roy Williams
Illustrations by Lalla Ward
Sweaters designed by Barbara Clarkson
from original sketches by Lalla Ward
Charts by Helen Clarkson

ISBN 0 283 99468 1

Photoset by
Rowland Phototypesetting Limited
Bury St Edmunds, Suffolk

Printed in Italy by
Imago Publishing Limited

CONTENTS

ACKNOWLEDGEMENTS

This is the chapter where I present the Golden Egg Awards to all the people who have given up their time to help me with *Fowl Knits*.

Golden Eggs (Ostrich-sized) go to my Friends who have made this book especially personal by modelling the sweaters: Jane and Caroline Blunden, Helena Burton, Sophie and Flora Daneman, Joanna David, Louise Jameson, Roxanna Panufnik, Sally Simpson, Angela Thorne and Gwen Watford.

A giant Thank You, the Golden Omelette Award, goes to Barbara Clarkson, without whose endless patience, unbelievable hard work, good humour and invaluable advice I couldn't have managed. The Silver Eggspoon Award goes to Helen Clarkson, for Best Technical Assistant, not to mention long-suffering model and tireless all-round helper.

The Bronze Turkey Award goes to Raffles.

Golden Egg Cups go to Colin Thomas, the Finest-Feathered Photographer I know, and to Rod Hedley Smith, the Make-up Artist with the Mostest. Also to Susie Slack, the Stylist.

The coveted Turquoise-Browed Motmot Award for Poet of the Year goes to Lord Birkett.

The Scrambled Egg Award is for Jo Edwards, my Editor, who unscrambled my over-enthusiastic (sometimes) contributions to some of the silliest ornithological rhymes ever concocted.

The Halcyon Award (see the Kingfisher chapter) goes to Heather Jeeves, for calming the occasional ripple and for being the best Literary Agent ever.

The Knitted Macaw Award goes to Colin Thorpe of Animal Fair for putting the Real McCaw in the picture.

Knitted Egg-Cosy Awards go to all the Knitters.

A Mirrored Egg Award goes to Andrew Logan, for making the Magpie brooches for me.

Finally, a special Wooden Egg Award goes to Mr Riemenschneider.

*I think the chicken must have come first
because it is hard to imagine God sitting on an egg.*

Unknown

INTRODUCTION

Let's get *Fowl Knits* off to an auspicious start: did you know that the word 'auspicious' comes from the Latin *avis* meaning bird and *spicere*, to see? The Romans used to try and foresee the outcome of events by watching the flight of birds or by looking at a bird's entrails.

Don't panic! I'm not suggesting that you chop up the budgie to find out if you are going to be able to knit one of these sweaters. I hope that the instructions will give you a good enough idea! I just thought that you might not know this useful piece of information and I've included in each chapter bits of poetry, fable, folklore or mythology to amuse you whilst you slave over the knitting needles. There are so many fascinating facts and fictions on an ornithological theme, although, needless to say, some of the birds I've chosen are much too obscure for any reference to be found in classical mythology or in literature, so you'll have to bear with the silly verses I've concocted myself to fill the gaps. My friend, Michael Birkett, has given me invaluable help with bird-rhymes where none were to be found – nowhere else could I track down a Turquoise-Browed Motmot poem but we've put all that to rights!

There are roughly 8,500 species of bird around today, so choosing thirty for this book proved quite tricky. I've included a mixture of the obvious pets – a Parrot, some Canaries, Budgies and a Cockatoo – some of the well-loved garden birds like Blue Tits and Robins and a few species you might not know, like the Quetzal and the Secretary Bird. I hope you will find something appropriate amongst this motley flock.

I've tried hard to cheer up the inevitable wordiness of most knitting books by giving you lots of illustrations along with the bits of rhyme and reason, to keep you entertained as you pore over the numbers and rows, tensions and abbreviations. Good luck with your fowl knitting. I hope you have as much fun wearing the sweaters as I have had doing this book.

Lalla

FOWL TECHNICALITIES

TENSION

The sweaters won t work out to the sizes we have given unless your tension is correct. Before starting a pattern, take the background yarn and the given needle size and cast on enough stitches to give you 15 centimetres (6½ inches). Work a square in stocking stitch (one row knit, one row purl). Measure 10 centimetres square (4 inches square) in the middle of your square and count your stitches and rows. If you have more stitches than specified, take smaller sized needles; if you have fewer, take larger sized ones. If you have the right number of stitches to 10 centimetres (4 inches) of knitting, your row tension should be approximately correct.

Please note that these are designer patterns and as such the needle sizes and tension may be different from that recommended by the spinner on the ball band.

YARN NOTES

These garments have been knitted in specified yarns to achieve the result illustrated, but any yarns can be used if they are the correct weight and knit to the given tension.

Please note that the amounts of yarn specified are based on average requirements and amounts given are therefore only approximate. They are measured in grammes. For the American knitter 1 ounce = 28.35 grammes.

SIZES

We've given two sizes for every garment, but the bird itself stays the same for both. If you are knitting the smaller size, follow the bold line at the edge of the chart; the broken line refers to the larger size. In the instructions, the first set of figures is for the smaller size and the second (in brackets) is for the larger. Where there is only one set of figures, this refers to both sizes.

WORKING FROM CHARTS

When working from charts, read K rows from right to left and

P rows from left to right, unless otherwise instructed in the pattern.

MOTIF KNITTING

So that each motif can be worked separately, use a separate ball of colour for each, or you may find it easier to wind off some yarn on to little 'fish' called jacquard bobbins (which you can find in most wool shops); you can anchor the yarn in the fish's mouth to stop it unravelling. Be very careful to twist the yarns together when changing colour, otherwise you will find yourself with a lacy design that you didn't intend! Where necessary, yarn can be carried over the wrong side of the work, but not for more than three stitches.

AN ALTERNATIVE WAY TO CAST OFF SHOULDERS

On some of the sweaters, you might prefer to cast the back and front shoulders off together. Obviously, this is only appropriate where there is no shoulder shaping. End each piece with the yarn at the armhole edge. Place right sides together. Using a third needle, knit two together (taking one stitch from the front and one from the back). Knit the next two stitches together in the same way and pass the stitch over, thus casting off one stitch. Repeat until all the stitches have been cast off and you have a neat, flat shoulder seam.

FINISHING OFF

Use a blunt-ended wool needle and darn the ends in along the colour join on the wrong side. Some yarns (for example, those used for the Avocet and the Penguins) may unravel and, to prevent this, dab the ends with a spot of colourless nail varnish.

EMBROIDERY

Swiss Embroidery (Fig. 1 – see page 12)
This is a useful way of working motifs and very small areas of colour such as the back of the Avocet chick or the spotty bits on the Budgerigars. It's also useful for covering up mistakes. It's best to do the Swiss embroidery when the garment is complete.

Use a tapestry (blunt-ended) needle and the colour you require. Bring the needle through from the back at the base of the stitch you wish to cover (1).
*Insert your needle from right to left behind the stitch above and draw the yarn through.

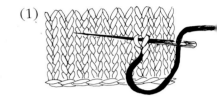

(1)

Take the needle to the back (at the point where you began) and bring it out again at the base of the next stitch you wish to cover (2).*
   Rep from * to *.

(2)

Swiss embroidery is normally worked from right to left. To cover a second row, complete the stitch as in (3) then bring the needle out at the base of the stitch in the line above.

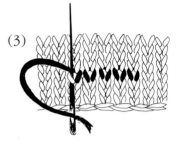

(3)

Turn the work upsidedown and repeat from * to *, *but* insert the needle behind the stitch *below*, as in (4).

To work a series of single stitches, complete each stitch, then bring the needle through to the front below the next stitch to be worked.

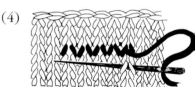

(4)

Other Embroidery

Chain stitch: (Fig. 2) Bring your needle through at A. Make a small loop and put the needle in again at A, holding the loop down. Bring the needle up again at B and pull the thread through keeping the loop under the needle point to form your first chain stitch. Repeat, putting the needle in again at B, coming up at C and holding the loop down under the needle point to form your second stitch.

Swiss embroidery diagrams from originals by Pingouin   Fig. 1

Fig. 2

Back stitch: (Fig. 3) Bring the thread through on the line you are following. Make a small backward stitch. Bring the needle through again a little in front of your first stitch. Make another stitch, putting your needle in at the point where it first came through.

Fig. 3

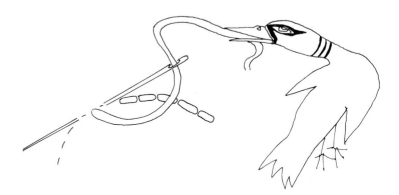

French knots: (Fig. 4) Bring the thread through at the required place. Hold the thread down with the left thumb. Encircle the needle twice with the thread, as in (1). Hold the thread firmly but not too tightly. Put the needle back in close to where the thread first emerged. Pull the thread through and secure for a single knot or continue to the position of the next knot (2).

Fig. 4

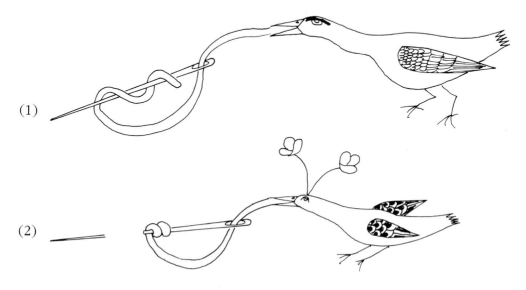

(1)

(2)

We have used Tootal Craft stranded embroidery cotton and we found that 3 strands were best, except for bold effects like the

claws on the Woodpecker, where we used all 6 strands.

Use your discretion with the embroidery. You will see from the photographs where we have put an eye or outlined a beak, such as on the Bald Eagle, or the head of the Griffon Vulture. Brown, black and white should be the only colours you will need.

PRESSING

Press very lightly on the wrong side of the work, following the instructions on the ball band. If you are using several qualities of yarn, use the coolest setting suggested. If pressing is not recommended for one of the yarns – don't!

NOTES FOR AMERICAN KNITTERS

Both metric and imperial measurements are given throughout the book, and we have included American needle sizes in the patterns. However, knitters on the other side of the Atlantic may find British knitting terminology and yarn names unfamiliar, so here are the translations:

UK	US
cast off	bind off
stocking stitch	stockinette stitch
tension	gauge
work straight	work even
Aran yarn	fisherman/medium weight yarn
chunky yarn	bulky yarn
double knitting	knitting worsted
4-ply yarn	lightweight yarn

NEEDLE CONVERSIONS

UK and Australia metric mm	2	2¼	2¾	3	3¼	3¾	4	4½	5	5½	6	6½	7	7½	8	9	10
UK and Australia original, Canada, S Africa	14	13	12	11	10	9	8	7	6	5	4	3	2	1	0	00	000
USA	00	0	1	2	3	4	5	6	7	8	9	10	10½	11	12	13	15

ABBREVIATIONS

alt	alternate
A,B,C,D,E,F,G,H,J,K	contrast colours
approx	approximately
beg	beginning
cm	centimetres
cont	continue
dec	decrease
DK	double knitting
foll	following
g	grammes
in	inches
inc	increase
K	knit
M1	make 1 stitch by picking up horizontal loop lying between stitch just worked and following stitch and working into the back of it
MC	main colour
mm	millimetres
P	purl
patt	pattern
RS	right side
rem	remaining
rep	repeat
sl	slip
st(s)	stitch(es)
st st	stocking stitch
tog	together
tbl	through back of loop
WS	wrong side
yfwd	yarn forward to make 1 stitch

Some abbreviations are only relevant to one pattern and are given under Special Abbreviations in the pattern text.

MANDARIN DUCK
Aix galericulata

The Mandarin Duck, unlike the Pheasant,
Is highly prized as a wedding present
In China, where this gorgeous fowl
Is considered wiser than the Owl.
This symbol of fidelity
Nests in a hole up in a tree –
It lives on snails and rice and seeds
And never, ever interbreeds.
The female wood duck *looks* the same
And bird buffs say 'What's in a name?'
But a Mandarin Duck's especially choosy
And won't be fobbed off with some floozy.
A faithful bird, he's stuck for life
With a *Mandarin* female for a wife.

MEASUREMENTS

To fit bust: 81–86(91–97)cm
[32–34(36–38)in].
Actual measurement: 106(116)cm
[41¾(45¾)in].
Length from shoulder: approx
61(63)cm [24(24¾)in].
Sleeve seam: 43(44)cm [17(17½)in].

MATERIALS

13(15) 50g balls of Wendy Dolce in
charcoal grey (468) – MC.
1 ball in each of beige (471) – A;
peach (472) – B.
1 50g ball of Wendy Family Choice DK
in each of yellow (903) – C; white
(212) – D; green (916) – E; black (247)
– F.
1 reel of gold sewing thread – G, to be
used together with B.
1 pair each of 3¼mm (US 3) and 4mm
(US 5) needles.
4 buttons.
2 spare needles.

TENSION

24sts and 32 rows to 10cm (4in) using
4mm (US 5) needles and st st using
MC.

NOTE

Yarns B and G are used together as
required.

FRONT

With 3¼mm (US 3) needles and MC,
cast on 101(113)sts and work in single
rib as follows:
1st row: (RS facing) K1, *P1, K1, rep
from * to end.
2nd row: P1, *K1, P1, rep from * to
end.
Rep these 2 rows until rib measures
8cm (3¼in), ending with a first row.
Increase row: Rib 5, M1, [rib 3(4), M1,
rib 4, M1] 13 times, rib 5(4).
[128(140)sts.]
Change to 4mm (US 5) needles and
starting with a K row, work 24 rows
straight in st st.
Joining in and breaking off colours as

required, cont in st st and colour patt
from chart, working between
appropriate lines for size required.
25th row: (RS facing) K68(74)MC,
K1C, K59(65)MC.
26th row: P58(64)MC, P2C,
P68(74)MC.
The chart is now placed.
Cont in patt from chart until 84 rows
of st st in all have been completed,
thus ending with a WS row.

Shape armholes

Keeping patt correct, cast off 4(5)sts at
beg of next 2 rows.
Dec 1st at each end of next 7(9) rows,
then foll 2(3) alt rows. [102(106)sts.]
Cont straight until 152(158) rows of st
st in all have been completed, thus
ending with a WS row.

Shape front neck

Next row: K44(45), and leave these sts
on a spare needle for left front, cast off
next 14(16)sts, K to end of row and
cont on this last set of 44(45) sts only
for right front.
Work 1 row.
Cast off 4sts at beg (neck edge) of next
row and foll alt row.
Dec 1st at neck edge on next 7 rows,
then on foll alt row. [28(29)sts.]
Work 3 rows.
Cast off all sts.
With WS facing rejoin MC to neck
edge of rem sts for left front, cast off
4sts, P to end. Work 1 row.
Cast off 4sts at beg (neck edge) of next
row, P to end.
Dec 1st at neck edge on next 8 rows.
Leave rem 28(29)sts on a spare needle
for shoulder border.

BACK

Work as given for front, omitting
colour patt and neck shaping, until 4
rows less than on front have been
worked to right shoulder, ending with
a WS row.

Shape back neck

Next row: K40(41), and leave these sts
on a spare needle for right back, cast
off next 22(24)sts, K to end of row and
cont on this last set of 40(41)sts only
for left back.
Work 1 row.
** Cast off 6sts at beg (neck edge) of
next row and foll alt row. [28(29)sts.]
**
Next row: (WS facing) P, and inc
3(4)sts evenly across.
Leave these 31(33)sts on a spare
needle for shoulder border.
With WS facing rejoin MC to neck
edge of rem sts for right back and
work as given for left back from ** to
**.
Work 1 row.
Cast off rem 28(29)sts.

SLEEVES (make 2)

With 3¼mm (US 3) needles and MC,
cast on 47(51)sts and work in single
rib as given for front welt for 6cm
(2¼in), ending with a first row.
Increase row: Rib 1(2), M1, [rib 2, M1,
rib 1, M1] 15(16) times, rib 1.
[78(84)sts.]
Change to 4mm (US 5) needles and
starting with a K row work in st st, inc
1st at each end of 5th row and then
every foll 4th row until there are
122(132)sts on the needle.
Now work straight until sleeve
measures 43(44)cm [17(17½)in] from
cast-on edge, ending with a WS row.

Shape top

Cast off 4(5)sts at beg of next 10 rows,
4sts at beg of foll 6 rows, 6sts at beg of
next 2 rows, then 7sts at beg of foll 2
rows.
Cast off rem 32sts fairly loosely.

NECKBAND

Join right shoulder seam.
With 3¼mm (US 3) needles and MC
and RS facing, pick up and K54(56)sts
evenly around front neck, then

47(49)sts evenly around back neck.
[101(105)sts.]
Starting with a 2nd row, work in
single rib as given for front welt for
5cm (2in).
Cast off fairly loosely ribwise.
Fold neckband in half to inside and
slip stitch loosely in position.

BACK SHOULDER BORDER
With 3¼mm (US 3) needles and MC
and RS facing, pick up and K6sts along
back edge of neckband, then
K31(33)sts from spare needle.
[37(39)sts.]
Starting with a 2nd row, work in
single rib as given for front welt for 6
rows.
Cast off fairly loosely ribwise.

FRONT SHOULDER BORDER
With 3¼mm (US 3) needles and MC
and RS facing, K28(29)sts from spare
needle, inc 3(4)sts evenly, then pick
up and K6sts up front edge of
neckband. [37(39)sts.]
Starting with a 2nd row, work in
single rib as given for front welt for 2
rows.
Buttonhole row: (WS facing) Rib 3,
[cast off 2sts, rib 6] 4 times, rib to end.
Next row: Rib, casting on 2sts over
cast-off sts on previous row. (4
buttonholes worked.)
Work 2 more rows in rib.
Cast off fairly loosely ribwise.

TO MAKE UP
Lay front shoulder border over back
shoulder border and catch neatly
together at armhole edge. Join side
and sleeve seams. With centre of
cast-off edges of sleeves to shoulder
seam/middle of shoulder borders,
sew sleeves carefully into armholes.
Sew on buttons to back shoulder
border to correspond with
buttonholes.
Embroider eye, using chain stitch and
a French knot, as shown.

EUROPEAN BEE-EATER
Merops apiaster

The rainbow bird is a gorgeous sight
As it flits through the air on a moonlit night;
Its legs are little and absurdly weak
But its tail is streamlined and its body sleek.

As it zig-zags about in a swarm of bees,
The Bee-eater picks them off with ease,
Swoops like a swallow amidst its prey
And the apiarist has lost the day.

The European Bee-eater's Carmine cousin
Gorges on locusts by the dozen
And African farmers are pleased as punch
That this insect pest is the Carmine's lunch.

The Jamaican Tody is related, too,
With the Cuckoo-roller and the Wood-hoopoe,
The Kingfisher, Kookaburra both fit in
With its Motmot relatives and Hornbill kin.

It catches insects on the wing
And who really cares if it can't quite sing?
Its tropical plumage amid the trees
Is a lovely sight, save to Europe's bees.

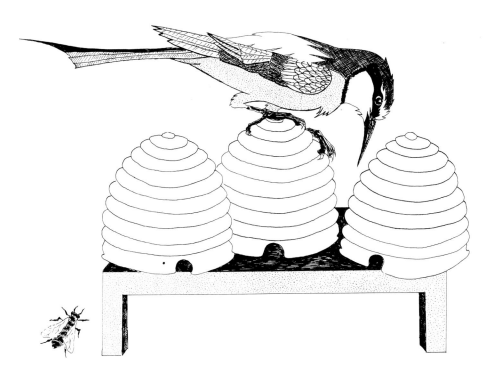

MEASUREMENTS

To fit bust: 81–86(91–97)cm
[32–34(36–38)in].
Actual measurement: 105(116)cm
[41¼(45¾)in].
Length from back neck: approx
60(63)cm [23½(24¾)in].
Sleeve seam: 43(44)cm [17(17½)in].

MATERIALS

9(11) 50g balls of Hayfield Grampian
DK in pale green (127) – MC.
1 ball in black (024) – E.
1 50g ball of Hayfield Lugano in each
of bright green (077) – A; turquoise
(052) – B; brown (066) – C; yellow
(079) – D.
1 pair each of 3¼mm (US 3) and 4mm
(US 5) needles.
Spare needle.

TENSION

22sts and 28 rows to 10cm (4in) using
4mm (US 5) needles and st st using
MC.

FRONT

With 3¼mm (US 3) needles and MC,
cast on 101(113)sts and work in single
rib as follows:
1st row: (RS facing) K1, *P1, K1, rep
from * to end.
2nd row: P1, *K1, P1, rep from * to
end.
Rep these 2 rows until rib measures
8cm (3¼in), ending with a first row. **
Increase row: Rib 8, M1, [rib 6(7), M1]
14 times, rib 9(7). [116(128)sts.]
Change to 4mm (US 5) needles and
starting with a K row, work 17 rows
straight in st st.
Joining in and breaking off colours as
required, cont in st st and colour patt
from chart, working between
appropriate lines for size required.
18th row: (WS facing) P10(16)MC,
P1A, P105(111)MC.
19th row: K104(110)MC, K1A,
K11(17)MC.
The chart is now placed.

Cont in patt from chart until 64 rows
of st st in all have been completed,
thus ending with a WS row.

Shape raglans

Keeping patt correct, cast off 2sts at
beg of next 2 rows.
3rd row: K1, K2tog, patt to last 3sts,
K2tog tbl, K1.
4th row: P.
5th row: K.
6th row: P.
Rep 3rd to 6th rows. [108(120)sts.]
Now rep 3rd and 4th rows only until
48(52)sts rem, ending with a 4th
row.

Shape front neck

Next row: (RS facing) K1, K2tog, K14
and leave these sts on a spare needle
for left front, cast off next 14(18)sts, K
to last 3sts, K2tog tbl, K1, and cont on
this last set of 16sts only for right
front.
Work 1 row.
*** Keeping raglan shaping as set, cast
off 4sts at neck edge on next row and
foll 2 alt rows.
Next row: Work 2tog and fasten off.
With WS facing rejoin MC to neck
edge of rem sts for left front and work
as for right front from *** to end.

BACK

Work as given for front to **.
Increase row: Rib 8, M1, [rib 7(8), M1]
12 times, rib 9. [114(126)sts.]
Change to 4mm (US 5) needles and
starting with a K row, work straight in
st st in MC only until back measures
the same as front to beg of raglan
shaping, ending with a WS row.

Shape raglans

Work as given for front until 34(38)sts
rem, ending with a WS row.
Cast off all sts.

RIGHT SLEEVE

With 3¼mm (US 3) needles and MC,
cast on 53(55)sts and work in single

rib as given for front welt for 5cm
(2in), ending with a first row.
Increase row: Rib 3(5), M1, [rib 3, M1,
rib 3(2), M1] 8(9) times, rib 2(5).
[70(74)sts.]
Change to 4mm (US 5) needles and
starting with a K row work in st st in
MC only, inc 1st at each end of 5th row
and then every foll 4th row until there
are 74(84)sts on the needle. Now inc
1st at each end of every foll 6th row
until there are 104(112)sts on the
needle.
Now work a few rows straight until
sleeve measures 43(44)cm
[17(17½)in] from cast-on edge,
ending with a WS row.

Shape raglans

Cast off 2sts at beg of next 2 rows.
3rd row: K1, K2tog, K to last 3sts,
K2tog tbl, K1.
4th row: P.
Rep the last 2 rows until 38sts remain,
ending with a WS row.
Next row: K1, K2tog, K15 and leave
these sts on a spare needle for front
section, cast off next 2sts, K to last 3sts,
K2tog tbl, K1, and cont on this last set
of 17sts for back section.
Dec at raglan edge as before and, **at
the same time,** dec 1st at neck edge
on foll 7 alt rows. [3sts.]
Next row: P3.
Next row: K2tog tbl, K1.
Next row: P2.
Next row: K2tog and fasten off.
With WS facing rejoin yarn to neck
edge of rem sts for front section and
dec at raglan edge as before and, **at
the same time,** dec 1st at neck edge
on next 10 rows. [2sts.]
Next row: P2.
Next row: K2tog and fasten off.

LEFT SLEEVE

Work as given for right sleeve until
64sts remain in raglan shaping,
ending with a RS row.
Joining in and breaking off colours as

required, cont in st st and colour patt
from chart.

Next row: P23MC, P2D, P39MC.

The chart is now placed.

Cont in patt from chart, still dec at
raglans as before until chart is
complete.

Cont to dec at raglans until 38sts rem,
ending with a WS row.

Next row: K1, K2tog, K15 and leave
these sts on a spare needle for back
section, cast off next 2sts, K to last 3sts,
K2tog tbl, K1, and cont on this last set
of 17sts for front section, and work as
given for front section of right sleeve.
With WS facing rejoin yarn to neck
edge of rem sts for back section, and
work as given for back section of right
sleeve.

NECKBAND

Join raglan seams, leaving left back
raglan open.

With 3¼mm (US 3) needles and MC
and RS facing, pick up and K 24sts
along edges of left sleeve top,
36(40)sts across front, 24sts along
edges of right sleeve top and finally
33(37)sts across back. [117(125)sts.]
Starting with a 2nd row, work in
single rib as for front welt for 5cm
(2in).

Cast off fairly loosely ribwise.

TO MAKE UP

Join rem raglan and neckband seam.
Fold neckband in half to inside and
slip stitch loosely in position. Join side
and sleeve seams. Embroider eye,
using chain stitch and a French knot,
as shown.

LEFT SLEEVE

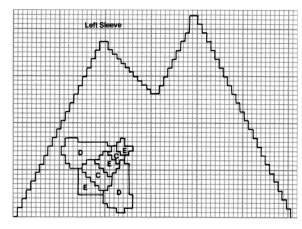

Centre

Centre

TURQUOISE-BROWED MOTMOT
Eumomota superciliosa

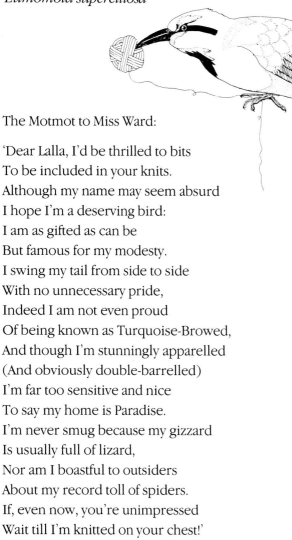

The Motmot to Miss Ward:

'Dear Lalla, I'd be thrilled to bits
To be included in your knits.
Although my name may seem absurd
I hope I'm a deserving bird:
I am as gifted as can be
But famous for my modesty.
I swing my tail from side to side
With no unnecessary pride,
Indeed I am not even proud
Of being known as Turquoise-Browed,
And though I'm stunningly apparelled
(And obviously double-barrelled)
I'm far too sensitive and nice
To say my home is Paradise.
I'm never smug because my gizzard
Is usually full of lizard,
Nor am I boastful to outsiders
About my record toll of spiders.
If, even now, you're unimpressed
Wait till I'm knitted on your chest!'
                                    Lord Birkett

Miss Ward to the Motmot:

'Dear Motmot, What-what can I say?
Except that you have made my day.
It's I who should be thrilled to bits
You want to be in *Fowl Knit-Knits*.
A knitting book without a Motmot
Wouldn't do, so thanks a lot-lot.'

MEASUREMENTS

To fit bust: 81–86(91–97cm)
[32–34(36–38)in].
Actual measurement: 105(116)cm
[41¼(45¾)in].
Length from back neck: approx
88(90)cm [34¾(35½)in].
Sleeve seam: 46cm [18in].

MATERIALS

14(16) 50g balls of Sirdar Sovereign
DK in pale grey (002) – MC.
1 ball in each of black (013) – A; beige
(033) – E.
1 50g ball of Sirdar Nocturne in each
of turquoise (565) – B; green (572) –
C; rust (510) – D.
1 pair each of 3¼mm (US 3) and 4mm
(US 5) needles.
Stitch holder.
Spare needle.
2 safety pins.

TENSION

22sts and 27 rows to 10cm (4in) using
4mm (US 5) needles and st st using
MC.

FRONT

With 3¼mm (US 3) needles and MC,
cast on 110(120)sts and work in K1,
P1, rib for 18cm (7in).
Increase row: Rib 10(11), M1, [rib
18(14), M1] 5(7) times, rib 10(11).
[116(128)sts.]
Change to 4mm (US 5) needles and
starting with a K row, work 15 rows
straight in st st.
Joining in and breaking off colours as
required, cont in st st and colour patt
from chart, working between
appropriate lines for size required.
16th row: (WS facing) P37(43)MC,
P4A, P75(81)MC.
17th row: K73(79)MC, K11A,
K32(38)MC.
The chart is now placed.
Cont in patt from chart, noting areas
which have to be worked in reversed
st st, until 86 rows of st st in all have

been completed, thus ending with a
WS row.

Shape raglans

Keeping patt correct, cast off 2(3)sts at
beg of next 2 rows.
3rd row: K1, K2tog, patt to last 3sts,
K2tog tbl, K1.
4th to 6th rows: Work in patt.
Rep 3rd to 6th rows 13(12) times
more **.
Now rep 3rd and 4th rows 15(20)
times, ending with a 4th row.
[54(56)sts.]

Shape front neck

Next row: (RS facing) K1, K2tog, K16,
and leave these sts on a spare needle
for left front, cast off next 16(18)sts, K
to last 3sts, K2tog tbl, K1, and cont on
this last set of 18sts only for right
front.
Work 1 row.
*** Keeping raglan shaping as set, cast
off 4sts at neck edge on next row, then
3sts at this edge on foll alt row.
Now dec 1st at neck edge on next 5
rows. [2sts.]
Next row: Work 2tog and fasten off.
With WS facing rejoin MC to neck
edge of rem sts for left front and work
as for right front from *** to end.

BACK

Work as given for front to ** omitting
colour patt.
Now rep 3rd and 4th rows until
40(42)sts remain, ending with a 4th
row.
Leave sts on a stitch holder.

RIGHT SLEEVE

With 3¼mm (US 3) needles and MC,
cast on 46(50)sts and work in K1, P1,
rib for 6cm (2¼in).
Increase row: Rib 2(4), M1, [rib 2, M1]
21 times, rib 2(4). [68(72)sts.]
Change to 4mm (US 5) needles and
starting with a K row work 4 rows in
st st.

Shape sides

Next row: (RS facing) K2, M1, K to last
2sts, M1, K2.
Work 3 rows in st st.
Rep last 4 rows until there are
104(108)sts on the needle, then cont
to inc in the same way on every foll
6th row from last inc until there are
114(118)sts on the needle.
Work a few rows straight until sleeve
measures 46cm (18in) from cast-on
edge, ending with a WS row.

Shape raglans

Cast off 2(3)sts at beg of next 2 rows.
3rd row: K1, K2tog, K to last 3sts,
K2tog tbl, K1.
4th row: P.
2nd size only:
5th and 6th rows: Work in st st.
Rep 3rd to 6th rows. [108sts.]
Both sizes:
Rep 3rd and 4th rows until 14sts rem,
ending with a 4th row. ****

Shape top

Next row: (RS facing) Cast off 4sts
(front edge), K7, K2tog tbl, K1.
Next row: P.
Next row: Cast off 3sts, K3, K2tog tbl,
K1.
Next row: P.
Leave rem 5sts on a safety-pin.

LEFT SLEEVE

Work as given for right sleeve to ****.
Complete to match right sleeve
reversing shaping at top.

NECKBAND

Join raglans, leaving left back raglan
open.
With 3¼mm (US 3) needles and MC
and RS facing, K across the 5sts from
left sleeve inc 1st at centre, pick up
and K16(17)sts down left sleeve top
and front neck, 18(20)sts across front,
16(17)sts up right front neck and
sleeve top, K across the 5sts from right
sleeve inc 1st at centre, then finally K
across the 40(42)sts from back inc 2sts

evenly. [104(110)sts.]
Work in K1, P1, rib for 5cm (2in).
Cast off fairly loosely ribwise.

TO MAKE UP
Join rem raglan and neckband seam.
Fold neckband in half to inside and

slip stitch loosely in position. Join side
and sleeve seams.
Embroider eye with a French knot.

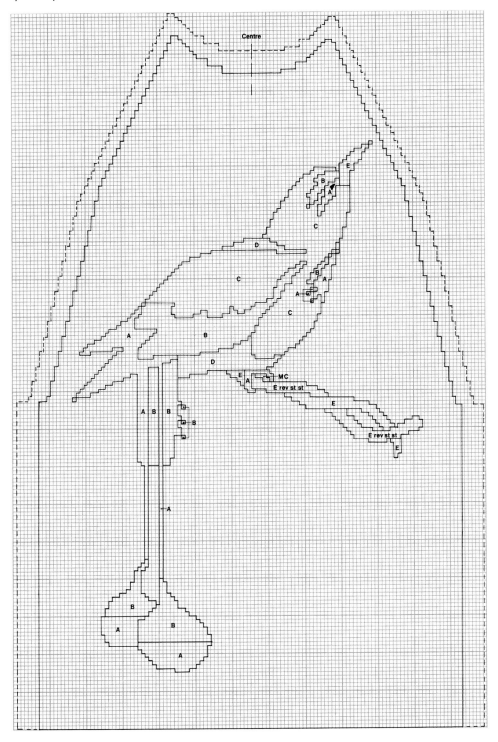

QUETZAL
Pharomachrus mocinno

The hardest thing, when writing verse about the wretched Quetzal
Is finding words to rhyme with it more apropos than 'pretzel'.
The problem, too, arises when you come to Guatemala –
The Quetzal lives there but it doesn't rhyme (as would koala).
To get away from these non-sequiturs: the knitty-gritty
Is that the Quetzal gave its name to Guatemala's second city;
It's their monetary unit and you'll find it on their seal;
It was hunted by the Aztecs with unprecedented zeal,
For, like modern Guatemalans, to the Aztec and the Maya
There was nothing in the world that you could value any higher
Than the Quetzal's tail feathers. It was worshipped and revered
And they called it Quetzalcoatl, feathered serpent. But they feared
That once captured, it would perish. So they always set it free –
Once they'd plucked its gorgeous plumage, they would let the poor bird be.
What a help it would have been to anxious Quetzals far and wide
If the Aztec ceremonial decorations had relied
On the skills of Aztec knitters. For a ceremonial sweater,
From the point of view of Quetzals, would have been a great deal better.

31

MEASUREMENTS

To fit bust: 81–86(91–97)cm
[32–34(36–38)in].
Actual measurement: 111(120)cm
[43¾(47¼)in].
Length from shoulder: approx
65(68)cm [25½(26¾)in].
Sleeve seam: 44(45)cm [17½(17¾)in].

MATERIALS

14(16) 50g balls of Pingouin Pingostar
in emerald (508) – MC.
1 ball in each of black (533) – A; red
(531) – B; brown (556) – C.
1 50g ball of Pingouin Intrigue in each
of black/green (08) – D; black/blue
(07) – E.
1 pair each of 3¾mm (US 4) and
4½mm (US 6) needles.
4 buttons.
Spare needle.

TENSION

18sts and 24 rows to 10cm (4in) using
4½mm (US 6) needles over diagonal
patt using MC.

BACK

With 3¾mm (US 4) needles and MC,
cast on 91(97)sts and work in single
rib as follows:
1st row: (RS facing) K1, *P1, K1, rep
from * to end.
2nd row: P1, *K1, P1, rep from * to
end.
Rep these 2 rows until rib measures
8cm (3¼in), ending with a first row.
Increase row: Rib 8(6), M1, [rib
15(12), M1] 5(7) times, rib 8(7).
[97(105)sts.]
Change to 4½mm (US 6) needles and
pattern as follows:
1st row: (RS facing) K1, [P1, K4] 6(8)
times, P1, K28(16), [P1, K4] 7(9) times,
P1, K1.
2nd row: P2, [K1, P4] 7(9) times, K1,
P26(14), [K1, P4] 6(8) times, K1, P2.
Cont in patt as set from chart, joining
in D on 10th(14th) row as indicated.
Joining in and breaking off colours as

required, cont in st st and reversed st
st and colour patt from chart, working
between appropriate lines for size
required, and work until 72 rows in
all have been completed, thus ending
with a WS row.

Shape armholes

Keeping patts correct, cast off 3(4)sts
at beg of next 2 rows.
Dec 1st at each end of next 3 rows,
then on foll 1(2) alt row(s).
[83(87)sts.]
Cont straight in patt from chart until
134(140) rows in all have been
completed, ending with a WS row.

Shape back neck

Next row: Patt 28(29)sts and leave
these sts on a spare needle for right
back, cast off next 27(29)sts, patt to
end and cont on this last set of
28(29)sts only for left back.
Work 1 row.
** Cast off 5sts at beg of next row.
Cast off rem 23(24)sts.
With WS facing rejoin MC to neck
edge of rem sts for right back and
work as given for left back from ** to
end.

LEFT FRONT

With 3¾mm (US 4) needles and MC,
cast on 45(49)sts and work in single
rib as given for back welt for 8cm
(3¼in), ending with a first row.
Increase row: Rib 9, M1, [rib 9(10),
M1] 3 times, rib 9(10). [49(53)sts.]
Change to 4½mm (US 6) needles and
pattern as follows: ***
1st row: (RS facing) *K4, P1, rep from
* to last 4(3)sts, K4(3).
2nd row: K1(0), *P4, K1, rep from * to
last 3sts, P3.
3rd row: K2, P1, *K4, P1, rep from * to
last 1(0)st, K1(0).
4th row: P2(1), K1, *P4, K1, rep from *
to last st, P1.
5th row: P1, *K4, P1, rep from * to last
3(2)sts, K3(2).

6th row: P4(3), *K1, P4, rep from * to
end.
7th row: K3, *P1, K4, rep from * to last
1(0)st, P1(0).
8th row: P1(0), K1, *P4, K1, rep from *
to last 2sts, P2.
Cont in patt as set, moving diagonals
1st to the right on every row and
creating new diagonals at the left as
required until 4 rows less than on
back have been worked to beg of
armhole shaping, ending with a WS
row.

Shape front slope

Keeping patt correct, dec 1st at end of
next row and at same edge on foll 3rd
row, thus ending at side edge.

Shape armhole

Cast off 3(4)sts at beg of next row.
Work 1 row.
Cont shaping front slope by dec 1st at
front edge on every foll 3rd row from
last dec, **at the same time**, cont
shaping armhole by dec 1st at
armhole edge on next 3 rows, then on
foll 1(2) alt row(s). [38(39)sts.]
Cont to dec at front edge on every foll
3rd row from last dec until 33(35)sts
rem, then on every foll 4th row until
23(24)sts rem.
Work 3(5) rows.
Cast off.

RIGHT FRONT

Work as given for left front to ***.
1st row: (RS facing) K4(3), *P1, K4,
rep from * to end.
2nd row: P3, *K1, P4, rep from * to last
1(0)st, K1(0).
3rd row: K1(0), P1, *K4, P1, rep from *
to last 2sts, K2.
4th row: P1, K1, *P4, K1, rep from * to
last 2(1)st(s), P2(1).
5th row: K3(2), P1, *K4, P1, rep from *
to end.
6th row: *P4, K1, rep from * to last
4(3)sts, P4(3).

7th row: P1(0), *K4, P1, rep from * to last 3sts, K3.

8th row: P2, K1, *P4, K1, rep from * to last 1(0)st, P1(0).

Cont in patt as set, moving diagonals 1st to the left on every row and creating new diagonals at the right as required, and finish to match left front reversing shapings.

LEFT SLEEVE

With 3¾mm (US 4) needles and MC, cast on 45(49)sts and work in single rib as for back welt for 6cm (2¼in), ending with a first row.

Increase row: Rib 2, M1, [rib 3, M1] 14(15) times, rib 1(2). [60(65)sts.]

Change to 4½mm (US 6) needles and patt as follows.

1st row: (RS facing) *P1, K4, rep from * to end. ****

2nd row: *K1, P4, rep from * to end.

3rd row: K3, *P1, K4, rep from * to last 2sts, P1, K1.

4th row: P2, K1, *P4, K1, rep from * to last 2sts, P2.

Cont in patt as set, moving diagonals 1st to the right on every row and creating new diagonals at the left as required.

***** **At the same time**, inc 1st at each end of 5th row and then every foll 4th row until there are 94(103)sts on the needle. Now inc 1st at each end of every foll 6th row until there are 98(107)sts on the needle, working inc sts into the patt on either side.

Now cont straight in patt until sleeve measures 44(45)cm [17½(18)in] from cast-on edge, ending with a WS row.

Shape top

Keeping patt correct, cast off 3(4)sts at beg of next 4 rows, then 5sts at beg of foll 12 rows.

Cast off rem 26(31)sts.

RIGHT SLEEVE

Work as for left sleeve to ****.

2nd row: P3, K1, *P4, K1, rep from * to last st, P1.

3rd row: K2, P1, *K4, P1, rep from * to last 2sts, K2.

4th row: P1, *K1, P4, rep from * to last 4sts, K1, P3.

Cont in patt as set, moving diagonals 1st to the left on every row and creating new diagonals at the right as required.

Complete as given for left sleeve from ***** to end.

RIGHT FRONT BORDER AND BUTTONHOLE BAND

With 3¾mm (US 4) needles and MC and RS facing, pick up and K73sts to start of right front slope and 66(70)sts to shoulder. [139(143)sts.]

Starting with a 2nd row work in single rib as given for back welt for 3 rows.

Buttonhole row: (RS facing) Rib 3, cast off 2sts, [rib 19, cast off 2sts] 3 times, rib to end.

Next row: Rib, casting on 2sts over cast-off sts on previous row. (4 buttonholes worked.)

Rib 2 rows.

Cast off fairly loosely ribwise.

LEFT FRONT BORDER AND BUTTON BAND

Joint left shoulder seam.

With 3¾mm (US 4) needles and MC and RS facing, and beg at right shoulder, pick up and K42(44)sts around back neck, 66(70)sts down left front slope and 73sts down left front. [181(187)sts.]

Starting with a 2nd row work in single rib as given for back welt for 7 rows.

Cast off fairly loosely ribwise.

TO MAKE UP

Join right shoulder seam and ends of borders. Join side and sleeve seams. With centre of cast-off edges of sleeves to shoulder seams, sew sleeves carefully into armholes. Sew on buttons to correspond with buttonholes.

Embroider eye, using chain stitch and a French knot, as shown.

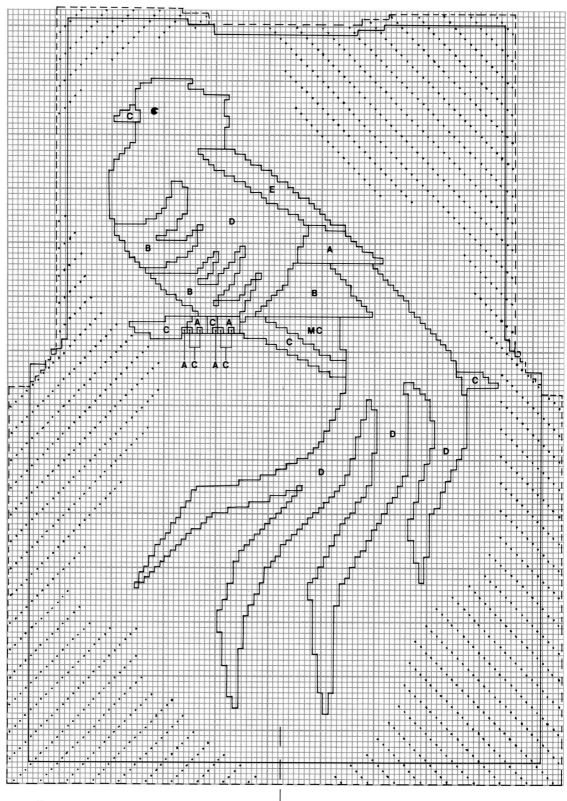

Key ⊡ = P on RS, K on WS of work   **Centre**

MUTE SWAN
Cygnus olor

The silver swan, who living had no note,
When death approached unlocked her silent throat
Leaning her breast against the reedy shore,
Thus sung her first and last, and sung nor more:
Farewell, all joys, oh death, come close mine eyes:
More geese than swans now live, more fools than wise.

Seventeenth-century madrigal

Oliver Goldsmith writes in *Animated Nature*, that the Swan 'has
not the smallest degree of melody, yet notwithstanding this, it
was the general opinion of antiquity that the Swan was the most
melodious bird. While Plato, Aristotle and Diodorus Siculus
believed the vocality of the Swan, Pliny and Virgil seem to doubt
that received opinion. It is probable the ancients had some
mythological meaning in ascribing melody to the Swan; and as
for the moderns, they scarcely deserve our regard.'

Richard the Lionheart is supposed to have brought the first
Mute Swans home with him from Cyprus after the third Crusade.
They were semi-domesticated as ornamental birds and eaten on
grand occasions.

By a statute of Edward IV, Swans were protected through
courts called swanmotes which kept control of the ownership of
every single swan, whether by the Crown or some corporation.
They are still marked now, by nicking
cygnets' beaks at the swan-upping
ceremony on the Thames every
summer. One nick means that
a swan belongs to the Dyers
Company, two nicks mean
that the Vintners own
that particular bird, and
all unmarked swans belong
to the Crown.

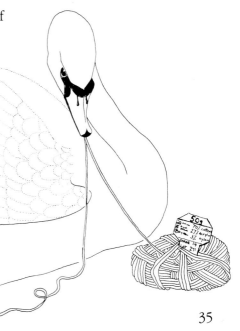

MEASUREMENTS

To fit bust: 81–86(91–97)cm
[32–34(36–38)in].
Actual measurement: 104(114)cm
[41(45)in].
Length from shoulder: approx
59(61)cm [23¼(24)in].
Sleeve seam: 43(44)cm [17(17½)in].

MATERIALS

10(11) 50g balls of Tootal Craft
Legend in peacock (704) – MC.
1 ball in black (714) – A.
1 50g ball of Tootal Craft Avalon in
each of orange (662) – B; aquamarine
(654) – C; mauve (657) – D; white
(651) – E.
1 pair each of 6mm (US 9) and 7mm
(US 10½) needles.
Spare needle.

TENSION

13sts and 16 rows to 10cm (4in) using
7mm (US 10½) needles and st st using
MC.

FRONT

With 6mm (US 9) needles and MC,
cast on 60(64)sts and work in K2, P2,
rib for 8cm (3¼in).
Increase row: Rib 6(5), M1, [rib 7(6),
M1] 7(9) times, rib 5. [68(74)sts.]
Change to 7mm (US 10½) needles
and starting with a K row, work 9 rows
straight in st st.
Joining in and breaking off colours as
required, cont in st st and colour patt
from chart, working between
appropriate lines for size required.
10th row: (WS facing) P52(55)MC,
P2A, P14(17)MC.
11th row: K14(17)MC, K3A,
K51(54)MC.
The chart is now placed.
Cont in patt from chart noting areas
which are to be worked in reversed st
st until 42 rows of st st in all have been
completed, thus ending with a WS
row.

Shape armholes

Keeping patt correct, cast off 2(3)sts at
beg of next 2 rows.
Now dec 1st at each end of next 5
rows, then on foll alt row. [52(56)sts.]
Cont straight in patt until 28(30) rows
have been worked from beg of
armhole shaping, thus ending with a
WS row.

Shape front neck

Next row: Patt 21(22), and leave these
sts on a spare needle for left front, cast
off next 10(12)sts, patt to end of row
and cont on this last set of 21(22)sts
only for right front.
Dec 1st at neck edge on next 6 rows,
then on foll alt row. [14(15)sts.]
Work 4 rows.
Cast off rem sts in patt.
With WS facing rejoin MC to neck
edge of rem sts for left front and work
in patt from chart, reversing neck
shaping.
Cast off rem 14(15)sts in patt.

BACK

Work as given for front, omitting
colour patt and neck shaping, until
14(16) rows less than on front have
been worked to cast-off shoulder
edge, ending with a WS row.
Joining in and breaking off colours as
required, cont in st st and colour patt
from chart, working between
appropriate lines for size required.
Next row: (RS facing) K19(21)MC,
K14E, K19(21)MC.
Next row: P15(17)MC, P20E,
P17(19)MC.
The chart is now placed.
Cont in patt from chart and work
10(12) rows more, thus ending with a
WS row.

Shape back neck

Next row: Patt 19(20), and leave these
sts on a spare needle for right back,
cast off next 14(16)sts, patt to end of
row and cont on this last set of

19(20)sts only for left back.
Work 1 row.
** Cast off 5sts at beg (neck edge) of
next row.
Cast off rem 14(15)sts.
With WS facing rejoin MC to neck
edge of rem sts for right back and
work as given for left back from ** to
end following chart.

SLEEVES (make 2)

With 6mm (US 9) needles and MC,
cast on 32(36)sts and work in K2, P2,
rib for 6cm (2¼in).
Increase row: Rib 3(5), M1, [rib 3, M1]
9 times, rib 2(4). [42(46)sts.]
Change to 7mm (US 10½) needles,
and starting with a K row, work in st st
and inc 1st at each end of 5th row and
then every foll 4th row until there are
60(66)sts on the needle. Now inc 1st
at each end of every foll 6th row until
there are 66(70)sts on the needle.
Work a few rows straight until sleeve
measures 43(44)cm [17(17½)in] from
cast-on edge, ending with a WS row.

Shape top

Cast off 2(3)sts at beg of next 2(8)
rows, and 3(4)sts at beg of foll 8(2)
rows. Cast off 6sts at beg of next 4
rows. Cast off rem 14sts.

POLO COLLAR

Join right shoulder seam, carefully
matching pattern.
With 6mm (US 9) needles and MC and
RS facing, pick up and K44(46)sts
evenly around front neck and
32(34)sts evenly around back neck.
[76(80)sts.]
Work in K2, P2, rib for 4cm (1¾in).
Using one 6mm (US 9) needle and
one 7mm (US 10½) needle, work a
further 6 rows in rib as set.
Change to 7mm (US 10½) needles
and cont in rib as set until collar
measures 20cm (8in).
Cast off fairly loosely ribwise.

TO MAKE UP

Join left shoulder seam and collar, reversing seam on collar for turn back.

Join side and sleeve seams. With centre of cast-off edges of sleeves to shoulder seams, sew sleeves carefully into armholes.

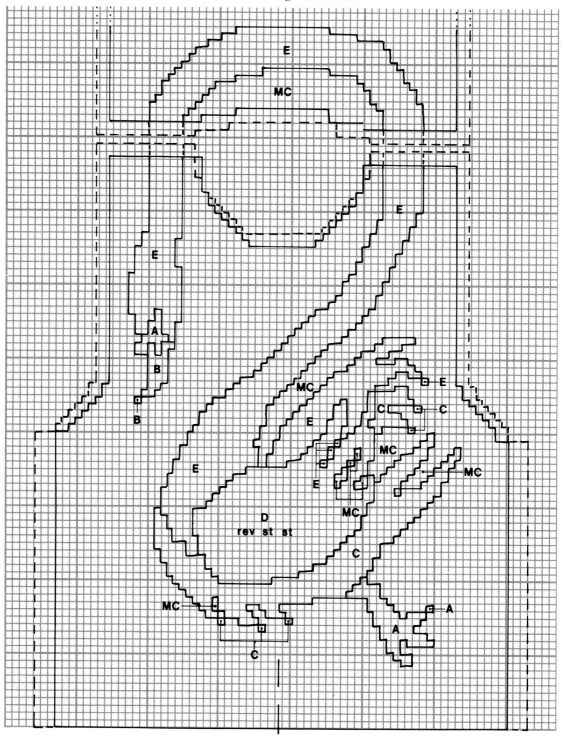

Centre

GREATER FLAMINGO
Phoenicopterus ruber

The Flamingo has the justest right to be placed among Cranes
and though it happens to be web-footed like birds of the Goose
kind, yet its height, figure and appetites entirely remove it from
that grovelling class of animal.

   A History of the Earth and Animated Nature Oliver Goldsmith

MEASUREMENTS

To fit bust: 81–86(91–97)cm [32–34(36–38)in].
Width from centre back to cuff: approx 61(65)cm [24(25½)in].
Length from shoulder: approx 65(67)cm [25½(26½)in].

MATERIALS

7(8) 50g balls of Phildar Luxe in navy (05) – MC.
1 ball in each of light pink (20) – A; medium pink (68) – B; dark pink (17) – C; white (10) – D; light grey (37) – E; dark grey (43) – F.
1 50g ball of Phildar Anouchka in white (10) – G.
1 pair each of 2¼mm (US 0) and 2¾mm (US 1) needles.
2¾mm (US 1) circular needle.
Spare needle.

TENSION

30sts and 40 rows to 10cm (4in) using 2¾mm (US 1) needles and st st using MC.

FRONT

With 2¼mm (US 0) needles and MC, cast on 138(150)sts and work in K1, P1, rib for 8cm (3¼in).
Increase row: Rib 6(9), M1, [rib 14(12), M1] 9(11) times, rib 6(9). [148(162)sts.]
Change to 2¾mm (US 1) needles and starting with a K row, work 12 rows straight in st st.

Shape sides

Inc 1st at each end of next row and then every foll 12th row until there are 158(172)sts on the needle, **at the same time**, when 22(28) rows of st st in all have been completed, joining in and breaking off colours as required, cont in st st and colour patt from chart.
Next row: (RS facing) K89(97)MC, K2E, K59(67)MC.
Next row: P59(67)MC, P2E, P89(97)MC.

The chart is now placed.
Cont in patt from chart until 62 rows of st st in all have been completed, now cont shaping sides by inc 1st at each end of next row and foll 33 alt rows, keeping chart correct; and changing to the 2¾mm (US 1) circular needle when necessary, and cont to work in **rows**. [226(240)sts.]
Inc 1st at each end of next row.
Next 2 rows: Cast on 2sts, patt to last st, inc in last st.
Rep last 2 rows 13(14) times more. [312(332)sts.]

Cast on 8(9)sts at beg of next 2 rows. [328(350)sts.]
Cont straight in patt from chart until 194(200)rows of st st in all have been completed, thus ending with a WS row.

Shape front neck

Next row: Patt 154(163) sts, and leave these sts on a spare needle for left front, cast off next 20(24)sts, patt to end of row and cont on this last set of 154(163)sts only for right front.
** Keeping patt correct, dec 1st at neck edge on next 16(18) rows, then at neck edge on foll 7(6) alt rows.
Work 2 rows.
Cast off rem 131(139)sts in patt.
With WS facing rejoin MC to neck edge of rem sts for left front and work as given for right front from ** to end, but working only 1 row before shoulder cast-off edge.

BACK

Work as given for front, omitting colour patt and neck shaping, until 200(206)rows of st st in all have been completed, thus ending with a WS row.
Joining in and breaking off colours as required, cont in st st and colour patt from chart.
Next row: (RS facing) K150(161)MC,

K19A, K159(170)MC.
Next row: P147(158)MC, P37A, P144(155)MC.
The chart is now placed.
Work 14 more rows in patt from chart.

Shape back neck

Next row: (RS facing) Patt 154(164) sts, and leave these sts on a spare needle for right back, cast off next 20(22)sts, patt to end of row and cont on this last set of 154(164)sts only for left back.
Work 1 row.
*** Keeping patt correct, cast off 5sts at beg (neck edge) of next row and foll 2 alt rows, then 4(5)sts at beg of foll 2 alt rows.
Cast off rem 131(139)sts in patt.
With WS facing rejoin MC to neck edge of rem sts for right back and work as given for left back from *** to end.

NECKBAND

Join right shoulder seam matching patt.
With 2¼mm (US 0) needles and MC and RS facing, pick up and K32(33)sts down left front neck, 21(25)sts across centre, 32(33)sts up right front neck, 23(24)sts down right back, 20(22)sts across centre, then 23(24)sts up left back. [151(161)sts.]
Next row: (WS facing) P1, *K1, P1, rep from * to end.
Next row: K1, *P1, K1, rep from * to end.
Rep the last 2 rows until rib measures 3cm (1¼in).
Cast off fairly loosely ribwise.

CUFFS (alike)

Join left shoulder seam and neckband matching patt.
With 2¼mm (US 0) needles and MC and RS facing, pick up and K84(90)sts evenly along lower edge of one sleeve. Work in K1, P1, rib for 3cm

(1¼in), ending with a WS row.
* **Next row:** In B, K.
Work 1 row in rib in B.
Next row: In MC, K.

Work 3 rows in rib in MC. *
Join in C and rep from * to * using C in place of B.
Cast off fairly loosely ribwise.

TO COMPLETE
Join side and underarm seams.
Embroider eyes, using chain stitch and French knots, as shown.

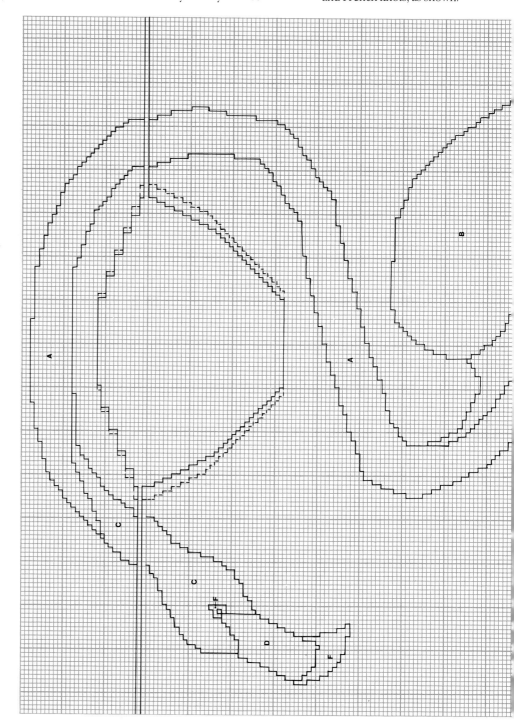

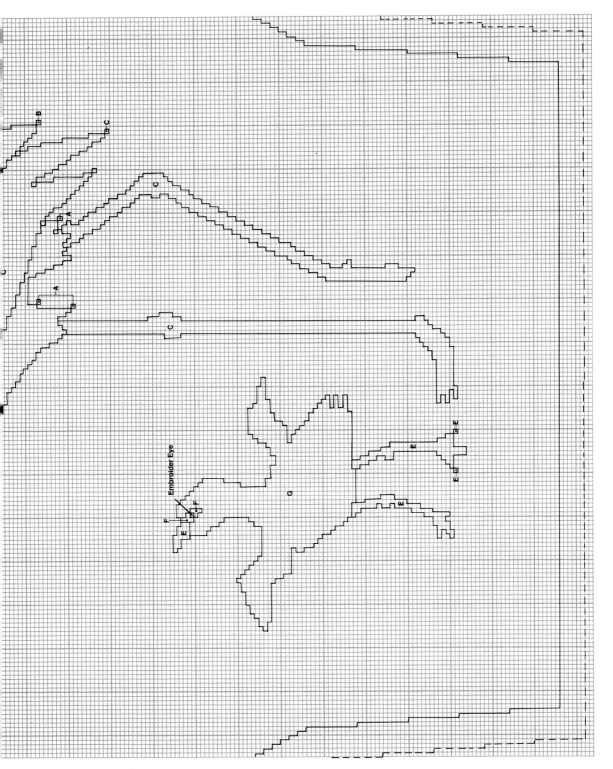

Centre

SULPHUR-CRESTED COCKATOO
Cacatua galerita

The Sulphur-crested Cockatoo
Looks like a punk and so would you
If you had sulphur-crested hair.
Instead of feathers everywhere
(Hardly a true punk's regalia)
This native of Australia,
To look the part, would be advised
To wear some leather, highly prized
By followers of King's Road chic.
A safety-pin stuck through his beak
Might add to his *je ne sais quoi*.
Cacatua galerita
(Family Cacatuidae)
Makes for King's Road on Saturday.
The Sulphur-crested folks down-under
Wait for news and while they ponder
The wheres and wherefores of their chick,
His mother, who is worried sick,
Passes the time, as is befitting,
Working her sorrows into her knitting.

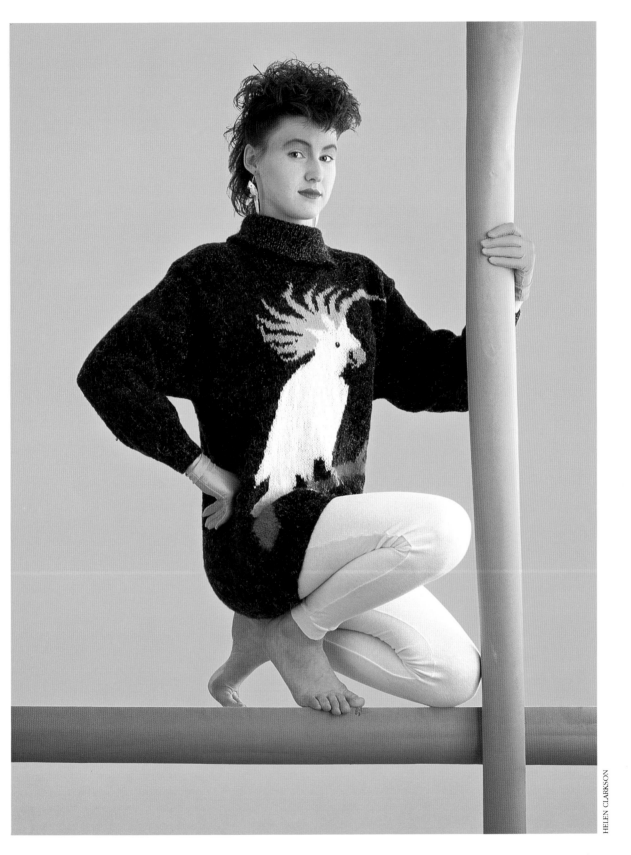

45

MEASUREMENTS

To fit bust: 81–86(91–97)cm
[32–34(36–38)in].
Actual measurement: 106(115)cm
[41¾(45¼)in].
Length from shoulder: approx
67(69)cm [26½(27)in].
Sleeve seam: 43(44)cm [17(17½)in].

MATERIALS

8(9) 50g balls of 3-Suisses Tossino in
black (07900) – MC.
1 ball in each of white (06000) – A;
yellow (07300) – B; blue/grey (07800)
– C.
1 50g ball of 3-Suisses Mohair 70 in
tan (0300) – D.
1 reel of gold glitter sewing thread –
E.
1 pair each of 3¼mm (US 3) and 4mm
(US 5) needles.
Spare needle.

TENSION

18sts and 26 rows to 10cm (4in) using
4mm (US 5) needles and st st using
MC.

NOTE

When working collar, E and MC are to
be used together.
When working crest, E and B are to be
used together.

FRONT

With 3¼mm (US 3) needles and MC,
cast on 88(96)sts and work in K1, P1,
rib for 8cm (3¼in).
Increase row: Rib 6, M1, [rib 11(12),
M1] 7 times, rib 5(6). [96(104)sts.]
Change to 4mm (US 5) needles and
joining in and breaking off colours as
required, cont in st st and colour patt
from chart, working between
appropriate lines for size required.
1st row: (RS facing) K79(83)MC, K9D,
K8(12)MC.
2nd row: P8(12)MC, P10D,
P78(82)MC.
The chart is now placed.
Cont in patt from chart until 82 rows

of st st in all have been completed,
thus ending with a WS row.

Shape armholes

Keeping patt correct, cast off 5(6)sts at
beg of next 2 rows. [86(92)sts.]
Cont in patt from chart until 140(146)
rows of st st in all have been
completed, thus ending with a WS
row.

Shape front neck

Next row: K34(36), and leave these sts
on a spare needle for left front, cast off
next 18(20)sts, K to end of row and
cont on this last set of 34(36)sts only
for right front.
Work 1 row.
** Dec 1st at neck edge on next 8(9)
rows, then on foll alt row. [25(26)sts.]
Work 3(2) rows.
Cast off rem sts.
With WS facing rejoin MC to neck
edge of rem sts for left front and work
as given for right front from ** to end.

BACK

Work as given for front, omitting
colour patt and neck shaping, until 6
rows less than on front have been
worked to cast-off shoulder edge,
ending with a WS row.

Shape back neck

Next row: K37(38), and leave these sts
on a spare needle for right back, cast
off next 12(16)sts, K to end of row and
cont on this last set of 37(38)sts only
for left back.
Work 1 row.
*** Cast off 4sts at beg (neck edge) of
next row and foll 2 alt rows.
Cast off rem 25(26)sts.
With WS facing rejoin MC to neck
edge of rem sts for right back and
work as given for left back from *** to
end.

SLEEVES (make 2)

With 3¼mm (US 3) needles and MC,
cast on 42(46)sts and work in K1, P1,

rib for 6cm (2¼in).
Increase row: Rib 5(4), [M1, rib 3, M1,
rib 3(4)] 6 times, rib 1(0). [54(58)sts.]
Change to 4mm (US 5) needles and
starting with a K row work in st st, inc
1st at each end of every foll 4th row
until there are 100(108)sts on the
needle.
Work a few rows straight until sleeve
measures 43(44)cm [17(17½)in] from
cast-on edge.
Place a marker at each end of last row.
Work a further 3(3.5)cm [1¼(1½)in]
straight.
Cast off all sts fairly loosely.

COLLAR

Join right shoulder seam.
With 3¼mm (US 3) needles and MC
and RS facing, pick up and K16(17)sts
down left front, 20(22)sts across
centre, 16(17)sts up right front, 15sts
down right back, 13(17)sts across
centre, then 15sts up left back.
[95(103)sts.]
Join in E, and using MC and E
together, work in rib as follows:
1st row: (WS facing) K2, *P1, K1, rep
from * to last st, K1.
2nd row: P2, *K1, P1, rep from * to last
st, P1.
Rep these 2 rows until collar
measures 3cm (1¼in).
Using one 3¼mm (US 3) needle, and
one 4mm (US 5) needle, work 6 rows
in rib as set.Change to 4mm (US 5)
needles and cont in rib as set until
collar measures 15cm (6in).
Cast off fairly loosely ribwise.

TO MAKE UP

Join left shoulder seam and first 3cm
(1¼in) of collar.
With centre of cast-off edges of sleeves
to shoulder seams, sew sleeves
carefully in position joining seam
above markers to cast-off sts at
underarm. Join side and sleeve seams.
Embroider eye, using chain stitch and
a French knot, as shown.

Centre

B·E

B·E

MC

C

C

MC

A

D

D

MC

C

D

MC

C

D

D

D

D

A

D

A

Key
□ }
⊠ } = MC

GREAT HORNED OWL
Bubo virginianus

A wise old Owl sat in an oak –
The more he heard, the less he spoke;
The less he spoke, the more he heard –
Why aren't we all like that wise old bird?

Anon

Did you know that the Owl was the favourite bird of the goddess Athena who, apart from being a warrior, was thought of as the goddess of reason and that that is why we refer to it as a wise old bird?

Or that, according to Ophelia, in *Hamlet*, the Owl was a 'baker's daughter'. According to legend, Christ was being given bread by the baker's wife, when her daughter scolded her for being over-generous. The miserable girl was promptly turned into an Owl for being so mean. Did you know that Owl broth is still given, in parts of Yorkshire, as a cure for whooping cough? Or that the Romans and Greeks believed that eating the heart of an Owl could cure blindness? Or that the Egyptians were terrified of Owls and thought they were harbingers of evil and death?

The Great Horned Owl is the biggest of the American Owls; so strong and ferocious that it's been known to prey on animals as big as domestic cats.

MEASUREMENTS

To fit bust: 81–86(91–97)cm
[32–34(36–38)in].
Actual measurement: 107(120)cm
[42(47¼)in].
Length from shoulder: approx
63(66)cm [24¾(26)in].
Sleeve seam: 46(47)cm [18(18½)in].

MATERIALS

16(18) 25g balls of Avocet Alpaca and
Mohair in white (103) – MC.
1 ball in each of gold (116) – A; black
(100) – B.
1 50g ball of Avocet Kazar in mottled
brown (1303) – C.
1 50g ball of Avocet Garbo in
brown/gold (702) – D.
1 50g ball of Avocet Cocoa in
brown/white (1000) – E.
1 pair each of 4½mm (US 6) and
5½mm (US 8) needles.
3 buttons for shoulder.
2 round buttons for eyes.
2 spare needles.

TENSION

16sts and 21 rows to 10cm (4in) using
5½mm (US 8) needles and st st using
MC.

FRONT

With 4½mm (US 6) needles and MC
cast on 84(92)sts and work in K2, P2,
rib for 10cm (4in).
Increase row: Rib 12(13), M1, [rib
60(22) M1] 1(3)time(s), rib 12(13).
[86(96)sts.]
Change to 5½mm (US 8) needles and
starting with a K row, work 8(14) rows
straight in st st.
Joining in and breaking off colours as
required, cont in st st and colour patt
from chart, working between
appropriate lines for size required.
Next row: (RS facing) K35(40)MC,
K1B, K15MC, K1B, K34(39)MC.
Next row: P34(39)MC, P1B, P15MC,
P1B, P35(40)MC.
The chart is now placed.

Cont in patt from chart until 94(100)
rows of st st in all have been
completed, thus ending with a WS
row.

Shape front neck

Next row: K34(38), and leave these sts
on a spare needle for left front, cast off
next 18(20)sts, K to end of row and
cont on this last set of 34(38)sts only
for right back.
** Work 1 row.
Dec 1st at neck edge on next 7 rows,
then on foll alt row. [26(30)sts.] **
Work 6 rows, thus ending at side
edge.
Cast off fairly loosely.
With WS facing rejoin MC to neck
edge of rem sts for left front and work
as given for right front from ** to **.
Work 1 row.
Leave rem 26(30)sts on a spare needle
for buttonhole border.

BACK

Work as given for front, omitting
colour patt and neck shaping, until
back measures 5 rows less than on
front to cast-off shoulder edge of right
shoulder, ending with a WS row.

Shape back neck

Next row: K36(40), and leave these sts
on a spare needle for right back, cast
off next 14(16)sts, K to end of row and
cont on this last set of 36(40)sts only
for left back.
Work 1 row.
*** Cast off 5sts at beg (neck edge) on
next row and foll alt row. ***
Leave rem 26(30)sts on a spare needle
for button border.
With WS facing rejoin MC to rem sts
for right back and work as given for
left back from *** to ***.
Cast off rem 26(30)sts fairly loosely.

SLEEVES (make 2)

With 4½mm (US 6) needles and MC,
cast on 40(44)sts. Join in A.
1st rib row: (RS facing) *K2A, P2MC,

rep from * to end.
2nd rib row: *K2MC, P2A, rep from *
to end.
Rep these 2 rows for 6cm (2¼in),
ending with a 2nd rib row. Break off
A.
Change to 5½mm (US 8) needles.
Increase row: (RS facing) K4(2), [M1,
K2(3), M1, K3] 7 times, K1(0).
[54(58)sts.]
Starting with a P row, cont in st st, inc
1st at each end of 5th(3rd) row and
then every foll 4th row until there are
92(98)sts on the needle.
Work straight until sleeve measures
46(47)cm [18(18½)in] from cast-on
edge, ending with a WS row.
Cast off all sts fairly loosely.

NECKBAND

Join right shoulder seam.
With 4½mm (US 6) needles and MC
and RS facing, and starting at left front
shoulder, pick up and K12(13)sts
down left front, 20(22)sts across
centre, 16(17)sts up right front, then
34(38)sts across back neck.
[82(90)sts.]
Join in A and work in double rib as
follows:
1st rib row: (WS facing) K2MC, *P2A,
K2MC, rep from * to end.
2nd rib row: P2MC, *K2A, P2MC, rep
from * to end.
Rep these 2 rows for 6cm (2¼in).
Cast off fairly loosely ribwise in
colours as set.
Fold neckband in half to inside and
slip stitch loosely in position.

BUTTON BORDER

With 4½mm (US 6) needles and MC
and RS facing, pick up and K5sts along
back edge of neckband, then
K26(30)sts from back shoulder inc
3sts evenly. [34(38)sts.]
Starting with a 2nd row, work in
double rib as for neckband, but
working in MC only.
Work 6 rows in rib.

Cast off fairly loosely ribwise.

BUTTONHOLE BORDER
With 4½mm (US 6) needles and MC
and RS facing, K26(30)sts from front
shoulder inc 3sts evenly, then pick up
and K5sts along front edge of
neckband. [34(38)sts.]
Work 2 rows in rib as given for button
border.
Buttonhole row: (WS facing) Rib 2,
[cast off 2sts, rib 8] 3 times, rib to end.
Next row: Rib, casting on 2sts over
cast-off sts on previous row. (3
buttonholes worked.)
Rib 2 rows.
Cast off fairly loosely ribwise.

TO MAKE UP
Lay buttonhole border over button
border and catch together at side
edge.
Place a marker at each side 28(30)cm
[11(12)in] below shoulder seams.
With centre of cast-off edges of sleeves
to shoulder/border seams sew sleeves
carefully in position between
markers. Join side and sleeve seams.
Sew on buttons to correspond with
buttonholes. Embroider eyes, using
chain stitch as shown, and sew a
button to centre of each eye.

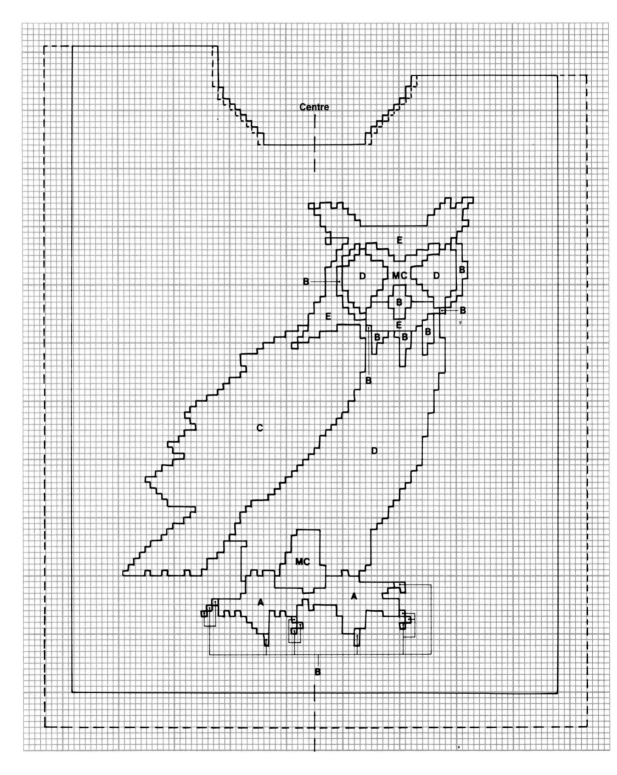

BALD EAGLE
Haliaeetus leucocephalus

The haughty eagle bird, of birds the best,
Before the feathers of her younglings grow,
She lifts them one by one from out their nest
To view the sun, thereby her own to know.
Those that behold it not with open eye,
She lets them fall, not able yet to fly.

from *My Love is Past* Thomas Watson

Aristotle and Pliny both wrote that the Eagle would force her
chicks to stare at the sun and that those whose eyes watered, or
who blinked, were thrown out of the nest.

Eagles were thought to seek out special stones which were put
in the nest to encourage the right egg-laying mood and the
Romans and Greeks believed that if a pregnant woman managed
to get hold of these stones, she would have an easy childbirth.

Shakespeare mentions the Eagle in lots of his plays:

I saw Jove's bird, the Roman eagle *Cymbeline*

. . . an eagle, madam,
Hath not so green, so quick, so fair an eye
As Paris hath *Romeo and Juliet*

More pity that the eagle should be mew'd
Whiles kites and buzzards prey at liberty *Richard III*

and from *Titus Andronicus*:

The eagle suffers little birds to sing,
And is not careful what they mean thereby,
Knowing that with the shadow of his wings
He can at pleasure stint their melody . . .

53

MEASUREMENTS

To fit bust: 81–86(91–97)cm [32–34(36–38)in].
Actual measurement: 105(116)cm [41¼(45¾)in].
Length from shoulder: approx 60(62)cm [23½(24½)in].
Sleeve seam: approx 45(46)cm [17¾(18)in].

MATERIALS

10(12) 50g balls of Sirdar Sovereign DK in beige (033) – MC.
1 ball in each of yellow (006) – A; white (051) – B; black (013) – C.
1 50g ball of Sirdar Nocturne in each of tan (568) – D; mottled brown (542) – E; rust (510) – F.
1 pair each of 3¼mm (US 3) and 4mm (US 5) needles.

TENSION

22sts and 27 rows to 10cm (4in) using 4mm (US 5) needles and st st using MC.

FRONT

With 3¼mm (US 3) needles and MC, cast on 102(112)sts and work in K1, P1, rib for 10cm (4in).
Increase row: Rib 6(4), M1, [rib 7, M1] 13(15) times, rib 5(3). [116(128)sts.]
Change to 4mm (US 5) needles and starting with a K row, work 5(11) rows straight in st st.
Joining in and breaking off colours as required, cont in st st and colour patt from chart, working between appropriate lines for size required.
Next row: (WS facing) P24(30)MC, P1C, P91(97)MC.
Next row: K33(39)MC, K2B, K57MC, K1C, K23(29)MC.
The chart is now placed.
Cont in patt from chart until 126(132) rows of st st in all have been completed, thus ending with a WS row.

Shape front neck

Next row: K50(56), turn.
Next row: Sl 1, P to end.
Next row: K43(49), turn.
Next row: Sl 1, P to end.
Next row: K36(42), turn.
Next row: Sl 1, P to end.
Next row: K across all 116(128)sts.

Shape 2nd side

Next row: P50(56), turn.
Next row: Sl 1, K to end.
Next row: P43(49), turn.
Next row: Sl 1, K to end.
Next row: P36(42), turn.
Next row: Sl 1, K to end.
** **Next row:** P across all sts, inc 5sts evenly. [121(133)sts.]

Yoke

Cont on same needles and work in single rib as follows:
Next row: (RS facing) K1, *P1, K1, rep from * to end.
Next row: P1, *K1, P1, rep from * to end.
Rep the last 2 rows until rib measures 5cm (2in), ending with a WS row.
Cast off fairly loosely ribwise.

BACK

Work as given for front, omitting colour patt, until back measures the same as front to beg of yoke, ending with a RS row, and omitting all neck shaping.
Complete as given for front from ** to end.

SLEEVES (make 2)

Beg at underarm and with 4mm (US 5) needles and MC, cast on 12(14)sts.

Shape side seam

1st row: (RS facing) K.
2nd row: Cast on 8 sts, P across these sts, P to end.
Rep these 2 rows until there are 84(86)sts on the needle.

Now cont straight in st st for a further 14.5(15.5)cm [5¾(6¼)in], ending with a RS row.
Next row: P, inc 5sts evenly across. [89(91)sts.]
Cont on same needles and work in single rib as given for yoke for 10cm (4in) ending with a RS row.
Next row: P and dec 5sts evenly across. [84(86)sts.]
Now starting with a K row, work 14.5(15.5)cm [5¾(6¼)in] in st st, ending with a RS row.

Shape side seam

Cast off 8sts at beg of next row and at this edge on foll 8 alt rows.
Work 1 row.
Cast off rem 12(14)sts.

TO MAKE UP

Using a flat seam join shoulders leaving 21(22)cm [8¼(8¾)in] free at centre. Place a marker at each side 26(27)cm [10¼(10¾)in] below shoulder seam. Insert sleeves between markers, matching rib and taking ½-st on sleeve rib and ½-st on yoke into seam.

CUFFS (alike)

With 3¼mm (US 3) needles and MC and RS facing, pick up and K66(70)sts evenly along lower edge of one sleeve.
Work in K1, P1, rib for 7cm (2¾in) ending with a WS row. Cast off fairly loosely ribwise.

TO COMPLETE

Join side and sleeve seams.
Embroider eye, using chain stitch and a French knot, as shown. Outline beak using back stitch and add a French knot for nostril.

FINCHES
Ploceidae

There's a Scarlet Finch, a Purple Finch, a Chestnut Mannikin,
And a type of wild canary which is known as a Siskin.
There are House Finches, Bullfinches, Goldfinches and Waxbills,
Silver-eyes and Firefinches, Parrot Finches, Crossbills –
The Crossbills come in two varieties, the Red and White
And they're vaguely linked to something called the European Twite.
The Bismark archipelago and northernmost Australia
Is where you'll find the Parrot Finch, in blue and green regalia.
There are circumpolar Redpolls in the Northern Hemisphere
And, among the old world seed-eaters, you'll find the Grenadier.
The small Red Avadavat has a rather curious name:
A corruption of Ahmadabad from whence this bird first came.
There are Yellow-bellied Waxbills and a red-cheeked Cordon Bleu,
There are Crimson-wings and Cut-throats and a type called Munia.
The Gouldian Finch is red faced and the Melba Finch is, too.
The Green-backed Twinspot's spotty and the Blue-bill's bill is blue.
There are stripes on Zebra Finches' tails and Tiger Finches' wings.
The Orange-cheek will chirp and tweet but hardly ever sings.
Bronze Mannikins and Hawfinches and Grosbeaks from Japan
Are not, perhaps, as well known as the Sparrow is to Man.
The tiny Locust Finch is quite a common little critter,
But like others on this list, perhaps unknown to you, the knitter.

MEASUREMENTS

To fit bust: 81–86(91–97)cm
[32–34(36–38)in].
Actual measurement: 104(114)cm
[41(45)in].
Length from shoulder: approx
59(61)cm [23¼(24)in].
Sleeve seam: approx 49(50)cm
[19¼(19¾)in].

MATERIALS

12(14) 50g balls of Patons Diploma
DK in black (6728) – MC.
1 ball in each of beige (6718) – A;
cerise (6737) – B; orange (6744) – C;
yellow (6736) – D; green (6733) – E;
red (6732) – F; turquoise (6734) – G;
purple (6735) – H; light green (6742)
– J; blue (6723) – K.
1 pair each of 3¼mm (US 3) and 4mm
(US 5) needles.
1 spare needle.

TENSION

22sts and 30 rows to 10cm (4in) using
4mm (US 5) needles and st st using
MC.

FRONT

With 4mm (US 5) needles and MC,
cast on 66(70)sts.
Break yarn and leave sts on a spare
needle.
Beg at right side seam and with 4mm
(US 5) needles and MC, cast on 46sts.
Starting with a K row, work 14(18)
rows straight in st st.

Shape armhole

Next row: (RS facing) K46, then K
across the 66(70)sts from spare
needle thus:
K30(34)MC, P3A, K33MC.
[112(116)sts.]
Work 0(4) rows in colours as set.
Joining in and breaking off colours as
required, cont in st st and colour patt
from chart, working between
appropriate lines for size required.
Next row: (WS facing) P25MC, P6B,
P2MC, K3A, P76(80)MC.

Next row: K76(80)MC, P3A, K9B,
K24MC.
The chart is now placed.
Cont in patt from chart, working
'perch' in reversed st st as shown,
until 31(33) rows of st st in all have
been completed from beg of armhole,
thus ending with a RS row.

Shape front neck

Keeping patt correct, dec 1st at beg of
next row and foll 9 alt rows.
[102(106)sts.]
Work 27(31) rows straight, thus
ending with a RS row.
Now inc 1st at neck edge on next row
and foll 9 alt rows. [112(116)sts.]
** Cont straight in colour patt from
chart until 31(33) rows in all have
been completed from end of neck
shaping, thus ending with a RS row.

Shape armhole

Next row: Cast off 66(70)sts, P to end.
[46sts.]
Work 14(18) rows straight on rem sts.
Cast off fairly loosely.

BACK

Work as given for front, but you will
be starting at left side seam, and
omitting colour patt, until back
measures the same as front to beg of
neck shaping, ending with a RS row.

Shape back neck

Dec 1st at beg of next row and at neck
edge on every foll 6th row until
108(112)sts rem.
Work 27(31) rows straight, thus
ending with a RS row.
Now inc 1st at neck edge on next row
and at neck edge on every foll 6th row
until there are 112(116)sts on the
needle.
Now work as for front from ** to end,
omitting colour patt.

RIGHT SLEEVE

With 3¼mm (US 3) needles and MC,
cast on 44(48)sts and work in K2, P2,

rib for 6cm (2¼in).
Increase row: Rib 5, M1, [rib 1, M1]
35(37) times, rib 4(6). [80(86)sts.]
Change to 4mm (US 5) needles and
starting with a K row work in st st, ***
at the same time, inc 1st at each end
of 5th row and then every foll 4th row
until there are 112(120)sts on the
needle.
Work 2 rows.
Joining in and breaking off colours as
required, cont in st st and colour patt
from chart, working between
appropriate lines for size required.
Next row: (WS facing) P91(95)MC,
P1A, P20(24)MC.
Next row: [Inc in first st, K19(23)MC],
P1A, [K90(94)MC, inc at last st].
**** Cont in patt from chart as now set,
working 'perch' in reversed st st as
shown, and at the same time, shape
sides by inc 1st at each end of every
foll 4th row until there are
134(142)sts on the needle.
Work 19 rows straight.
Cast off all sts fairly loosely.

LEFT SLEEVE

Work as given for right sleeve to ***.
Now inc 1st at each end of 5th row.
[82(88)sts.]
Joining in and breaking off colours as
required, cont in st st and colour patt
from chart, working between
appropriate lines for size required.
6th row: (WS facing) P38(41)MC, P1H,
P43(46)MC.
7th row: K40(43)MC, K1H, K1MC,
K2H, K38(41)MC.
Now work as given for right sleeve
from **** to end.

WELTS (Back and front alike)

With 3¼mm (US 3) needles and MC
and RS facing, pick up and
K92(100)sts evenly along lower edge
of either back or front.
Work in K2, P2, rib for 8cm (3¼in).
Cast off fairly loosely ribwise.

NECKBAND

Join right shoulder seam.
With 3¼mm (US 3) needles and MC
and RS facing, pick up and K64(68)sts
evenly around front neck, then
52(56)sts evenly around back neck.
[116(124)sts.]
Work in K2, P2, rib for 5cm (2in).
Cast off fairly loosely ribwise.

TO MAKE UP

Join left shoulder seam and neckband.
Fold neckband in half to inside and
slip stitch loosely in position. With
centre of cast-off edges of sleeves to
shoulder seams, sew sleeves carefully
into armholes joining top 4.5(6)cm
[1¾(2¼)in] of sleeves to straight edge
of armhole. Join side and sleeve
seams. Embroider eyes, using chain
stitch and French knots, as shown.
Using chain stitch and back stitch,
embroider legs and feet as shown.

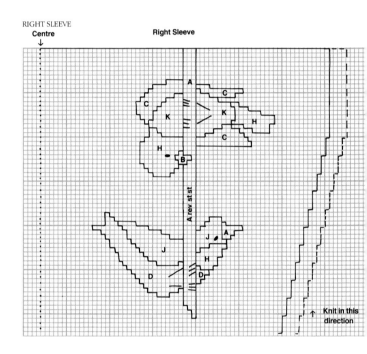

RIGHT SLEEVE

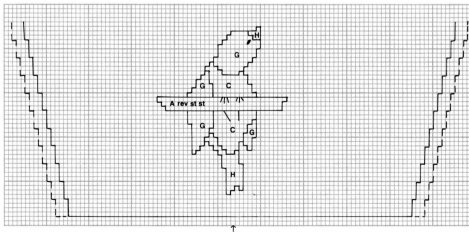

LEFT SLEEVE

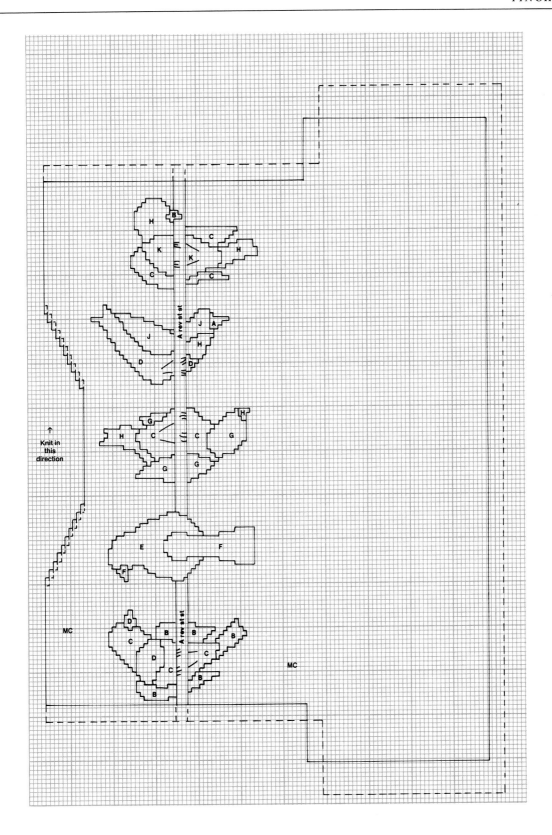

ROBINS
Erithacus rubecula

Goodbye, goodbye to summer!
For summer's nearly done;
The garden smiling faintly,
Cool breezes in the sun;
Our thrushes now are silent,
Our swallows flown away –
But Robin's here, in coat of brown,
With ruddy breast-knot gay.
Robin, Robin Redbreast,
O Robin dear!
Robin sings so sweetly
In the falling of the year.

Bright yellow, red, and orange,
The leaves come down in hosts;
The trees are Indian princes,
But soon they'll turn to ghosts;
The scanty pears and apples
Hang russet on the bough;
It's autumn, autumn, autumn late,
'Twill soon be winter now.
Robin, Robin Redbreast,
O Robin dear!
And what will this poor Robin do?
For pinching days are near.

The fireside for the cricket,
The wheatstack for the mouse,
When trembling night-winds whistle
And moan all round the house;
The frosty ways like iron,
The branches plumed with snow –
Alas! in winter dead and dark
Where can poor Robin go?
Robin, Robin Redbreast,
O Robin dear!
And a crumb of bread for Robin,
His little heart to cheer.

Robin Redbreast
William Allingham

63

MEASUREMENTS

To fit bust: 81–86(91–97)cm
[32–34(36–38)in].
Actual measurement: 101(110)cm
[39¾(43¼)in].
Length from shoulder: approx
60(62)cm [23½(24½)in].
Sleeve seam: 34(35)cm [13½(13¾)in].

MATERIALS

13(14) 50g balls of Robin Diamante
DK in pale blue (5904) – MC.
1 ball in each of red (5917) – A; brown
(5935) – B; white (5901) – C; pink
(5932) – D.
1 pair each of 3¼mm (US 3) and 4mm
(US 5) needles.
3¼mm (US 3) circular needle.
Spare needle.
1 button.

TENSION

22sts and 30 rows to 10cm (4in) using
4mm (US 5) needles and st st using
MC.

FRONT

With 3¼mm (US 3) needles and MC,
cast on 99(105)sts and work in single
rib as follows:
1st row: (RS facing) K1, *P1, K1, rep
from * to end.
2nd row: P1, *K1, P1, rep from * to
end.
Rep these 2 rows until rib measures
10cm (4in), ending with a first row.
Increase row: Rib 2(4), M1, [rib 8(6),
M1] 12(16) times, rib 1(5).
[112(122)sts.]
Change to 4mm (US 5) needles and
starting with a K row, work 15 rows
straight in st st.
Joining in and breaking off colours as
required, cont in st st and colour patt
from chart, working between
appropriate lines for size required.
16th row: (WS facing) P31(36)MC,
P2B, P79(84)MC.
17th row: K63(68)MC, K2B, K16MC,
K1B, K30(35)MC.

The chart is now placed.
Cont in patt from chart until 84 rows
of st st in all have been completed,
thus ending with a WS row.

Divide for V neck

Next row: K54(59), K2tog, turn and
leave rem 56(61)sts on a spare needle
for right front and cont on first set of
55(60)sts only for left front.
** Dec 1st at neck edge on every foll
3rd row until 34(37)sts rem.
Work 2 rows, thus ending at side
edge.
Cast off.
With RS facing rejoin MC to neck edge
of rem sts for right front, K2tog, K to
end of row.
Now work as for first side from ** to
end, but working 3 rows before
shoulder cast-off edge.

BACK

Work as given for front, omitting
colour patt and neck shaping, until
back measures 4 rows less than on
front to cast-off shoulder edge, ending
with a WS row.

Shape back neck

Next row: K46(51), and leave these sts
on a spare needle for right back, cast
off next 20sts, K to end of row and
cont on this last set of 46(51)sts only
for left back.
Work 1 row.
*** Cast off 6(7)sts at beg (neck edge)
of next row and foll alt row.
Cast off rem 34(37)sts.
With WS facing rejoin MC to neck
edge of rem sts for right back and
work as given for left back from *** to
end.

SLEEVES (make 2)

With 3¼mm (US 3) needles and MC,
cast on 47(51)sts and work in single
rib as given for front welt for 6cm
(2¼in), ending with a first row.
Increase row: Rib 3(1), M1, [rib 3, M1,
rib 4, M1] 6(7) times, rib 2(1).

[60(66)sts.]
Change to 4mm (US 5) needles and
starting with a K row, work in st st, inc
1st at each end of every foll 3rd row
until there are 112(120)sts on the
needle.
Work a few rows straight until sleeve
measures 34(35)cm [13½(13¾)in]
from cast-on edge, ending with a WS
row.
Cast off all sts fairly loosely.

FRONT STRAP

With 3¼mm (US 3) needles and MC,
cast on 15sts and work in rib as
follows:
1st row: (RS facing) K2, [P1, K1] 6
times, K1.
2nd row: P2, [K1, P1] 6 times, P1.
Rep these 2 rows once.
Buttonhole row: (RS facing) Rib 6,
cast off 3sts, rib to end.
Next row: Rib, casting on 3sts over
cast-off sts on previous row.
Cont in rib until strap measures 14cm
(5½in) from cast-on edge.
Cast off fairly loosely ribwise.

NECKBAND

Join right shoulder seam.
With the 3¼mm (US 3) circular
needle and RS facing and MC, and
starting at left front shoulder, pick up
and K68(72)sts down left front, 1st at
centre of V (mark this st), 68(72)sts up
right front, then 50(52)sts across back.
[187(197)sts.]
Work backwards and forwards in
rows as follows:
1st row: (WS facing) *P1, K1, rep from
* to within 2sts of marked st, P2tog, P1,
P2tog tbl, ** K1, P1, rep from ** to end.
2nd row: K1, *P1, K1, rep from * to
within 2sts of marked st, P2tog tbl, K1,
P2tog, K1, ** P1, K1, rep from ** to
end.
Rep these 2 rows until neckband
measures 3cm (1¼in), ending with a
first row.

Cast off loosely ribwise, dec at V as before.

TO MAKE UP
Join left shoulder seam and neckband. Place markers at each side of back and front 25(27)cm [10(10½)in] below shoulders. With centre of cast-off edges of sleeves to shoulder seams, sew sleeves in position between markers. Join side and sleeve seams. Sew cast-off edge of front strap to wrong side of pick-up row on right front, placing lower edge approx 6cm (2¼in) above point of V. Sew a button to right side of pick-up row on left front to correspond with buttonhole. Embroider eyes, using chain stitch and French knots, as shown. Embroider feet.

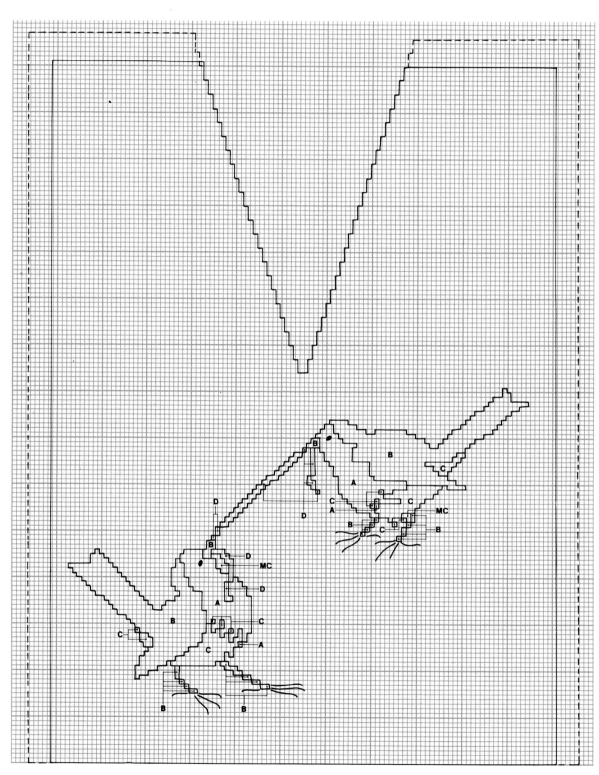

Centre

TOCO TOUCAN
Ramphastos toco

Oh, Toucan! What an odd-shaped bill
It looks like a canoe.
I'm sure you have some hidden skill
That's known to none but you.

I've seen you flying through the trees,
Along the Orinoco –
Tell me your secret, won't you please,
My dear *Ramphastos toco*?

The scientists are much confused
About your outsized beak –
Don't take offence or feel abused
But face it, you're a freak.

Now, come on, Toucan, tell us why
This feat of engineering,
Honeycomb-light so you can fly,
Should so impair your steering?

I've even heard you're wont to roam,
You and the Toucanets,
Into an unsuspecting home
And tease domestic pets!

Poor Toucan! I'm an utter fool
And scientists are twits –
Your beak evolved to hold the wool
And help us with *Fowl Knits*!

MEASUREMENTS

To fit bust: 81–86(91–97)cm [32–34(36–38)in].
Width from centre back to cuff: approx 56(58.5)cm [22(23)in].
Length from shoulder: approx 60(63)cm [23½(24¾)in].

MATERIALS

10(12) 50g balls of Scheepjeswol Linnen Brillant in coral (7579) – MC.
1 ball in each of black (7560) – A; red (7576) – B; white (7561) – C; yellow (7580) – D.
1 pair each of 3¾mm (US 4) and 4½mm (US 6) needles.
4½mm (US 6) circular needle.
Spare needle.

TENSION

20sts and 24 rows to 10cm (4in) using 4½mm (US 6) needles and st st using MC.

FRONT

With 3¾mm (US 4) needles and MC, cast on 91(99)sts and work in single rib as follows:
1st row: (RS facing) K1, *P1, K1, rep from * to end.
2nd row: P1, *K1, P1, rep from * to end.
Rep these 2 rows until rib measures 8cm (3¼in), ending with a first row.
Increase row: Rib 9, M1, [rib 12(10), M1] 6(8) times, rib 10. [98(108)sts.]
Change to 4½mm (US 6) needles and starting with a K row, work 2 rows in st st.
Joining in and breaking off colours as required, cont in st st and colour patt from chart, working between appropriate lines for size required.
3rd row: (RS facing) K51(56)MC, K1A, K25MC, K1A, K20(25)MC.
4th row: P13(18)MC, P1A, P6MC, P1A, P15MC, P1A, P9MC, P1A, P51(56)MC.
The chart is now placed.
Cont in patt from chart, **at the same time**, when 20 rows of st st in all have

been completed, shape sides by inc 1st at each end of next row and foll 13 alt rows. [126(136)sts.]
Now inc 1st at each end of next 17 rows. [160(170)sts.]
Cast on 10sts at beg of next 4 rows, changing to the 4½mm (US 6) circular needle when necessary, and cont to work in **rows**. [200(210)sts.]
Cont straight in patt on these sts until 116(122) rows of st st in all have been completed, thus ending with a WS row.

Shape front neck

Next row: K92(95), and leave these sts on a spare needle for left front, cast off next 16(20)sts, K to end of row and cont on this last set of 92(95)sts only for right front.
Work 1 row.
** Cast off 4sts at beg (neck edge) of next row and foll alt row, thus ending at side edge.
Next row: Cast off 25(26)sts, work to end.
Next row: Cast off 4sts, work to end.
Rep last 2 rows.
Cast off rem 26(27)sts.
With WS facing rejoin MC to neck edge of rem sts for left front and work as given for right front from ** to end.

BACK

Work exactly as given for front, but omitting colour patt.

NECK BORDERS (alike)

With 3¾mm (US 4) needles and RS facing and MC, pick up and K59(63)sts evenly around back/front neck edge.
Starting with a 2nd row, work in single rib as given for front welt for 4cm (1¾in).
Cast off fairly loosely ribwise.

TO MAKE UP

Join shoulder seams, leaving neck borders free. Place front neck border over back at shoulders and slip stitch ends neatly to right side of pick up

row along back. Sew ends of back neck border to wrong side of front in the same way.

CUFFS (alike)

With 3¾mm (US 4) needles and RS facing and MC, pick up and K41(45)sts evenly along lower edge of one sleeve.
Starting with a 2nd row, work in single rib as given for front welt for 6cm (2¼in).
Cast off fairly loosely ribwise.

TO COMPLETE

Join side and underarm seams.

COMMON PUFFIN
Fratercula arctica

What a wonderful bird is the Puffin,
The clown with the over-sized beak –
He can fill it with lobster and stuff in
Enough food to last him a week.

Unknown

71

MEASUREMENTS

To fit bust: 81–86(91–97)cm [32–34(36–38)in].
Actual measurement: 105(116)cm [41¼(45¾)in].
Length from shoulder: approx 59(60)cm [23¼(23½)in].
Sleeve seam: 43(44)cm [17(17½)in].

MATERIALS

12(14) 50g balls of Robin Reward DK in yellow (1347) – MC.
1 ball in each of red (1350) – A; black (1307) – B; white (1312) – C; blue (1313) – D.
1 pair each of 3¼mm (US 3) and 4mm (US 5) needles.
2 spare needles.

TENSION

22sts and 30 rows to 10cm (4in) using 4mm (US 5) needles and st st using MC.

FRONT

With 3¼mm (US 3) needles and MC cast on 101(111)sts and work in single rib as follows:
1st row: (RS facing) K1, *P1, K1, rep from * to end.
2nd row: P1, *K1, P1, rep from * to end.
Rep these 2 rows until rib measures 5cm (2in), ending with a first row. **
Increase row: Rib 2(8), M1, [rib 7(6), M1] 14(16) times, rib 1(7). [116(128)sts.]
Change to 4mm (US 5) needles and starting with a K row, work 16 rows straight in st st.
Joining in and breaking off colours as required, cont in st st and colour patt from chart, working between appropriate lines for size required.
17th row: (RS facing) K82(88)MC, K1B, K33(39)MC.
18th row: P32(38)MC, P2B, P82(88)MC.
The chart is now placed.
Cont in patt from chart until 134(138)

rows of st st in all have been completed, thus ending with a WS row.

Shape front neck

Next row: K51(56), and leave these sts on a spare needle for left front, cast off next 14(16)sts, K to end of row, and cont on this last set of 51(56)sts only for right front.
Work 1 row.
*** Cast off 3sts at beg (neck edge) of next row and foll alt row.
Cast off rem 45(50)sts.
With WS facing rejoin MC to neck edge of rem sts for left front and work as for right front from *** to end.

BACK

Work as given for front to **.
Increase row: Rib 3, M1, [rib 5, M1] 19(21) times, rib 3. [121(133)sts.]
Change to 4mm (US 5) needles and patt as follows:
1st, 3rd and 5th rows: (RS facing) K.
2nd row and every alt row: P.
7th row: K4(5), [P3tog, K3tog, P3tog] into next 3sts, *K7, [P3tog, K3tog, P3tog] into next 3sts, rep from * to last 4(5)sts, K4(5).
9th, 11th and 13th rows: K.
15th row: K9(10), *[P3tog, K3tog, P3tog] into next 3sts, K7, rep from * to last 2(3)sts, K2(3).
16th row: P.
These 16 rows form the patt for the back and are repeated as required.
Cont straight in patt as set until back measures the same as front to cast-off shoulder edge, ending with a WS row.
Cast off all sts fairly loosely.

LEFT SLEEVE AND SADDLE YOKE

With 3¼mm (US 3) needles and MC cast on 45(49)sts and work in single rib as given for front welt for 5cm (2in), ending with a first row.
Increase row: Rib 6(8), M1, [rib 2, M1] 17 times, rib 5(7). [63(67)sts.]
Change to 4mm (US 5) needles and

starting with a K row, work 6 rows in st st, inc 1st at each end of 3rd row. [65(69)sts.]
Now work in patt as for back as follows:
7th row: (RS facing) Inc in first st, K5(7), [P3tog, K3tog, P3tog] into next 3sts, *K7, [P3tog, K3tog, P3tog] into next 3sts, rep from * to last 6(8)sts, K5(7), inc in last st.
Cont in patt as now set working as for back, **at the same time**, inc 1st at each end of every foll 4th row until there are 117(121)sts on the needle, working inc sts into the patt.
Now work straight until sleeve measures 43(44)cm [17(17½)in] from cast-on edge, ending with a WS row.

Shape top

Keeping patt correct, cast off 42(44)sts at beg of next 2 rows. [33sts.]
Work straight in patt until saddle extension measures 16(18)cm [6¼(7)in] from cast-off sts, ending with a WS row. **

Shape neck

Next row: Patt 13, and leave these sts on a spare needle for back, cast off next 9sts, patt to end of row and cont on this last set of 11sts only for front.
Work 1 row.
*** **2nd size only**
Dec 1st at inside edge on next row and foll 2 alt rows.
Both sizes: Dec 1st at inside edge on next 9(6) rows. [2sts.]
Work 1 row.
Work 2tog and fasten off.
With WS facing rejoin MC to rem 13sts for back and **** work 3 rows.
Dec 1st at inside edge on next row and every foll 4th row until 9sts remain.
Work straight until back section measures 10(10.5)cm [4(4¼)in] from beg of neck shaping, ending with a WS row.
Leave sts on a spare needle.

RIGHT SLEEVE AND SADDLE YOKE

Work as given for left sleeve to **.

Shape neck

Next row: (RS facing) Patt 11, and leave these sts on a spare needle for front, cast off next 9sts, patt to end of row and cont on last set of 13sts only for back.

Work as given for left sleeve from **** to end.

With WS facing rejoin MC to rem sts for front and work as given for left sleeve from *** to end.

COLLAR

With 3¼mm (US 3) needles and MC, cast on 141(147)sts and work in single rib as follows:

1st row: (RS facing) K2, *P1, K1, rep from * to last st, K1.

2nd row: P2, *K1, P1, rep from * to last st, P1.

Rep these 2 rows 4 times more.

Shape collar

Next row: Rib to last 6sts, turn.

Next row: Sl 1, rib to last 6sts turn.

Cont in this way working 6sts fewer on next 8 rows.

Next row: Sl 1, rib to end.

Cont in rib across all sts until collar measures 14cm (5½in) measured up centre.

Cast off fairly loosely ribwise.

TO MAKE UP

Join saddle yoke at centre back by grafting or casting off sts together. Place a marker at each side of back and front 19(20)cm [7½(8)in] below cast-off shoulder edges. Join front above markers to the 42(44) cast-off sts at front edge of each sleeve, then join top of front to straight edge of sleeve extension, matching end of neck shaping. Join top of back to straight edge of back sleeve extension, then join back above markers to cast-off sts at sleeve top. Join side and sleeve seams. Place a marker at each side of front neck 5cm (2in) from centre. Sew cast-on edge of collar into neck opening, beg and ending at markers [thus overlapping collar 10cm (4in) at centre] so that right side of collar lies over left and K2 at each end lies to front.

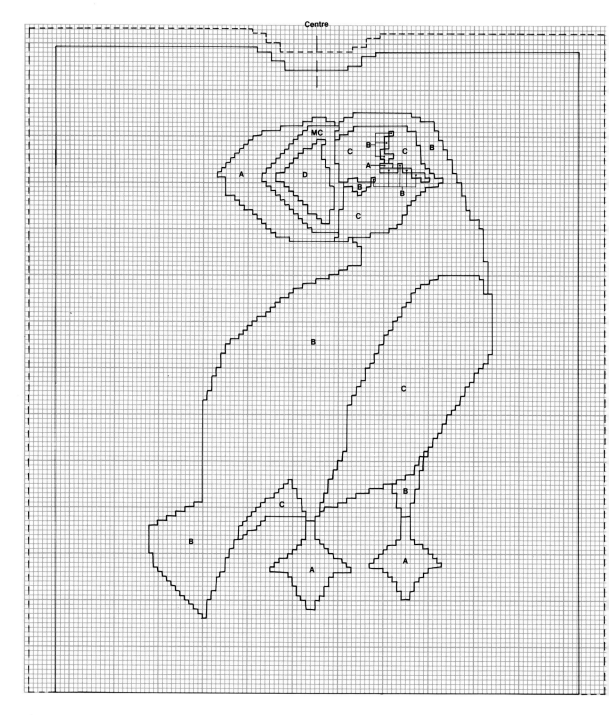

PHEASANT
Phasianus colchicus

The Gallinaceous family,
To which this bird belongs,
Is not renowned especially
For singing lovely songs –

But when it comes to looking nice
The Pheasant's unsurpassed –
Except, perhaps, in Paradise,
It leaves the rest out-classed.

The Ring-necked and the Tragopan
And Lady Amherst, too,
The Fireback, Reeves and Impeyan
To name a paltry few.

The Brown-eared Pheasant's ears are white –
Confusing? Yes, I know.
The Golden is a gorgeous sight,
It's head and back aglow,

And Argonauts, it's often thought,
First brought this bird to Greece.
The origin, it's sometimes taught
Of Jason's Golden Fleece.

MEASUREMENTS

To fit bust: 81–86(91–97)cm
[32–34(36–38)in].
Actual measurement: 105(112)cm
[41¼(44)in].
Length from shoulder: approx
90(92)cm [35½(36¼)in].
Sleeve seam: 43(44)cm [17(17½)in].

MATERIALS

10(12) 50g balls of Patons Beehive DK
in ecru (6002) – MC.
1 ball in each of black (6194) – B;
beige (6058) – C; pale blue (6154) –
D; white (6000) – E; dark green (6095)
– F; scarlet (6196) – G.
1 50g ball of Patons Pageant DK in
speckled browns (6486) – A.
1 pair each of 3¼mm (US 3) and 4mm
(US 5) needles.
Spare needle.

TENSION

22sts and 30 rows to 10cm (4in) using
4mm (US 5) needles and st st using
MC.

FRONT

With 3¼mm (US 3) needles and MC,
cast on 99(107)sts and work in single
rib as follows:
1st row: (RS facing) K1, *P1, K1, rep
from * to end.
2nd row: P1, *K1, P1, rep from * to
end.
Rep these 2 rows until rib measures
20cm (7¾in), ending with a first
row.
Increase row: Rib 7(9), M1, [rib
14(15), M1] 6 times, rib 8.
[106(114)sts.]
Change to 4mm (US 5) needles and
starting with a K row, work in st st, inc
1st at each end of 19th row and then
every foll 20th row until there are
116(124)sts on the needle, **at the
same time**, when 52 rows of st st in all
have been completed, joining in and
breaking off colours as required, cont
in st st and colour patt from chart,

working between appropriate lines
for size required.
53rd row: (RS facing) K8(12)MC, K1A,
K101(105)MC.
54th row: P100(104)MC, P1A,
P9(13)MC.
The chart is now placed.
Cont in patt from chart, shaping sides
as set, until 138 rows of st st in all have
been completed, thus ending with a
WS row.

Shape armholes

Keeping patt correct, cast off 4(5)sts at
beg of next 2 rows.
Dec 1st at each end of next 5 rows,
then foll 3(4) alt rows. [92(96)sts.]
Cont straight until 60(66) rows of st st
have been worked from beg of
armhole shaping, thus ending with a
WS row.

Shape front neck

Next row: K34(36), and leave these sts
on a spare needle for left front, cast off
next 24sts, K to end of row and cont
on this last set of 34(36)sts only for
right front.
** Dec 1st at neck edge on next 6(8)
rows, then foll 2(1) alt row(s).
[26(27)sts.]
Work 2 rows, thus ending at armhole
edge.

Shape shoulder

Cast off 13(14)sts at beg of next row.
Work 1 row.
Cast off rem 13sts.
With WS facing rejoin MC to neck
edge of rem sts for left front and work
as for right front from ** to end, but
working only 1 row before shoulder
shaping, thus ending at armhole edge.

BACK

Work as given for front, shaping sides
as for front, but omitting colour patt
and neck shaping, until 4 rows less
than on front have been worked to
beg of shoulder shaping, ending with
a WS row.

Shape back neck

Next row: K38(39), and leave these sts
on a spare needle for right back, cast
off next 16(18)sts, K to end of row and
cont on this last set of 38(39)sts only
for left back.
Work 1 row.
*** Cast off 6sts at beg (neck edge) on
next row and foll alt row, thus ending
at armhole edge.

Shape shoulder

Cast off 13(14)sts at beg of next row.
Work 1 row.
Cast off rem 13sts.
With WS facing rejoin MC to neck
edge of rem sts for right back and
work as for left back from *** to end.

SLEEVES (make 2)

With 3¼mm (US 3) needles and MC,
cast on 55(59)sts and work in single
rib as given for front welt for 5cm
(2in), ending with a first row.
Increase row: Rib 3, M1, [rib 6(5), M1,
rib 4, M1] 5(6) times, rib 2. [66(72)sts.]
Change to 4mm (US 5) needles and
starting with a K row work in st st, inc
1st at each end of 5th row and then
every foll 6th row until there are
82(88)sts on the needle. Now inc 1st
at each end of every foll 4th row until
there are 106(114)sts on the needle.
Work straight until sleeve measures
43(44)cm [17(17½)in] from cast-on
edge, ending with a WS row.

Shape top

Cast off 4(5)sts at beg of next 2 rows,
3sts at beg of foll 14(16) rows, 4sts at
beg of next 8 rows.
Cast off rem 24sts fairly loosely.

NECKBAND

Join right shoulder seam.
With 3¼mm (US 3) needles and MC
and RS facing, pick up and K16(17)sts
down left front neck, 26sts across
front, 16(17)sts up right front neck,
14sts down right back, 17(19)sts
across back, then finally 14sts up left

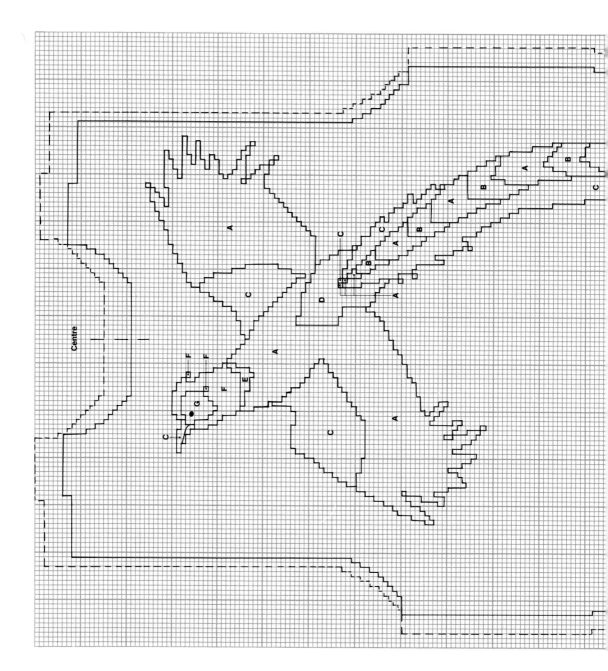

back neck. [103(107)sts.]
Starting with a 2nd row, work in
single rib as given for front welt for
5cm (2in).
Cast off fairly loosely ribwise.

TO MAKE UP
Join left shoulder seam and neckband.
Fold neckband in half to inside and
slip stitch loosely in position. Join side
and sleeve seams. With centre of
cast-off edges of sleeves to shoulder
seams, sew sleeves carefully into
armholes. Embroider eye, using chain
stitch and a French knot, as shown.
Outline beak using back stitch.

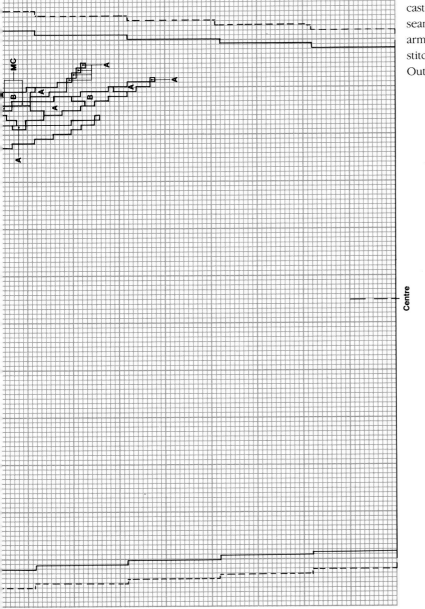

CUCKOO
Cuculus canorus

O blithe new-comer! I have heard,
I hear thee and rejoice,
O cuckoo! Shall I call thee bird,
Or but a wandering voice?

While I am lying on the grass
Thy twofold shout I hear,
From hill to hill it seems to pass
At once far off, and near.

Though babbling only to the vale,
Of sunshine and of flowers,
Thou bringest unto me a tale
Of visionary hours.

Thrice welcome, darling of the spring!
Even yet thou art to me
No bird, but an invisible thing,
A voice, a mystery;

The same whom in my schoolboy days
I listened to; that cry
Which made me look a thousand ways
In bush, and tree, and sky

To seek thee did I often rove
Through woods and on the green;
And thou wert still a hope, a love;
Still longed for, never seen.

And I can listen to thee yet;
Can lie upon the plain
And listen, till I do beget
That golden time again.

O blessed bird! the earth we pace
Again appears to be
An unsubstantial, faery place;
That is fit home for thee!

To the Cuckoo
William Wordsworth

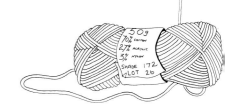

MEASUREMENTS

To fit bust: 81–86(91–97)cm [32–34(36–38)in].
Actual measurement: 105(113)cm [41¼(44½)in].
Length from shoulder: approx 61(62)cm [24(24½)in].
Sleeve seam: 43(44)cm [17(17½)in].

MATERIALS

9(10) 100g balls of Twilleys Pegasus 8-ply cotton in red (20) – MC.
1 ball in each of white (1) – A; black (79) – B.
1 50g ball of Twilleys Denim in each of grey (655) – C; charcoal (668) – D.
1 pair each of 3¼mm (US 3) and 4mm (US 5) needles.
Spare needle.

TENSION

19sts and 28 rows to 10cm (4in) using 4mm (US 5) needles and st st using MC.

FRONT

With 3¼mm (US 3) needles and MC, cast on 86(92)sts and work in K1, P1, rib for 10cm (4in).
Increase row: Rib 4(1), M1, [rib 6, M1] 13(15) times, rib 4(1). [100(108)sts.]
Change to 4mm (US 5) needles and starting with a K row, work 32 rows straight in st st.
Joining in and breaking off colours as required, cont in st st and colour patt from chart, working between appropriate lines for size required.
33rd row: (RS facing) K60(64)MC, K15D, K25(29)MC.
34th row: P24(28)MC, P18D, P58(62)MC.
The chart is now placed.
Cont in patt from chart until 68 rows of st st in all have been completed, thus ending with a WS row.

Shape armholes

Keeping patt correct, cast off 5(6)sts at beg of next 2 rows. [90(96)sts.]
Cont straight in patt until 130(134) rows of st st in all have been

completed, thus ending with a WS row.

Shape front neck

Next row: K39(41), and leave these sts on a spare needle for left front, cast off next 12(14)sts, K to end of row and cont on this last set of 39(41)sts only for right front.
Work 1 row.
** Cast off 4sts at beg (neck edge) on next row, then 3sts at beg of foll alt row.
Now dec 1st at neck edge on next 7 rows. [25(27)sts.] Work 1 row, thus ending at armhole edge.

Shape shoulder

Cast off 13(14)sts at beg of next row.
Work 1 row.
Cast off rem 12(13)sts.
With WS facing rejoin MC to neck edge of rem sts for left front and work as given for right front from ** to end.

BACK

Work as given for front, omitting colour patt and neck shaping, until 4 rows less than on front have been worked to beg of shoulder shaping, ending with a WS row. [90(96)sts.]

Shape back neck

Next row: K37(39), and leave these sts on a spare needle for right back, cast off next 16(18)sts, K to end of row and cont on this last set of 37(39)sts only for left back.
Work 1 row.
*** Cast off 6sts at beg (neck edge) of next row and foll alt row, thus ending at armhole edge.

Shape shoulder

Cast off 13(14)sts at beg of next row.
Work 1 row.
Cast off rem 12(13)sts.
With WS facing rejoin MC to neck edge of rem sts for right back and work as given for left back from *** to end.

SLEEVES (make 2)

With 3¼mm (US 3) needles and MC, cast on 40(42)sts and work in K1, P1, rib for 7cm (2¾in).
Increase row: Rib 2(1), M1, [rib 2, M1] 18(20) times, rib 2(1). [59(63)sts.]
Change to 4mm (US 5) needles and work in patt as follows:
1st row: (RS facing) K.
2nd row: P1(0), K3, *P3, K3, rep from * to last 1(0)st, P1(0).
These 2 rows form the patt for the sleeves and are repeated as required.
Cont in patt, **at the same time**, inc 1st at each end of 5th row and then every foll 6th row until there are 75(79)sts on the needle. Now inc 1st at each end of every foll 4th row until there are 99(105)sts on the needle, working inc sts into the patt.
Work a few rows straight in patt until sleeve measures 43(44)cm [17(17½)in] from cast-on edge.
Place a marker at each end of last row. Work a further 2.5(3)cm [1(1¼)in] in patt. Cast off fairly loosely.

NECKBAND

Join right shoulder seam.
With 3¼mm (US 3) needles and MC and RS facing, pick up and K47(51)sts evenly around front neck, then 40(42)sts evenly around back neck. [87(93)sts.]
Starting with a 2nd patt row, work 13 rows in patt as given for sleeves working as for 2nd size.
Cast off fairly loosely

TO MAKE UP

Join left shoulder seam and neckband. Fold neckband in half to inside and slip stitch loosely in position. With centre of cast-off edges of sleeves to shoulder seams, sew sleeves carefully in position joining seam above markers to cast-off sts at underarm.
Join side and sleeve seams.
Embroider eye, using back stitch and French knots, as shown.

82

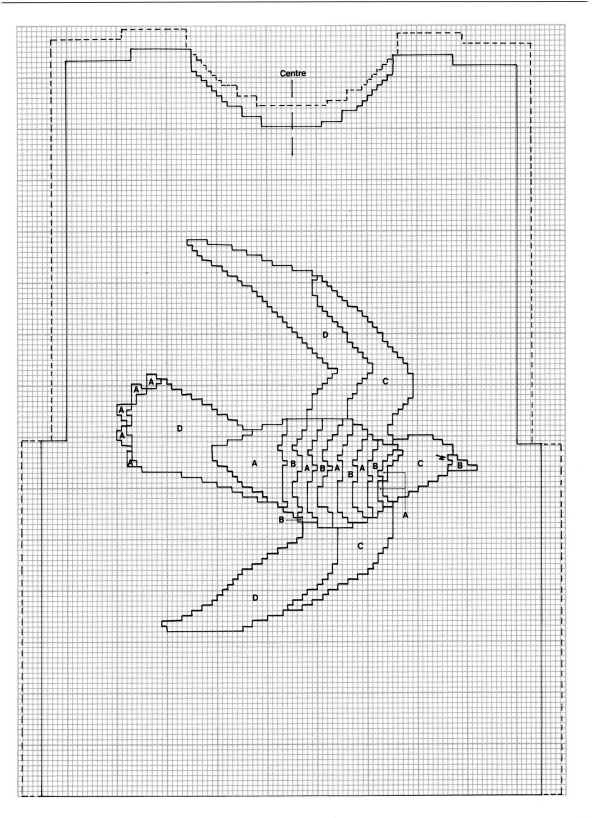

Centre

AVOCET

Recurvirostra avosetta

Avocets feed in mud and silt.
Related to the black-winged stilt,
They wade in shallows, where they're hogs
For molluscs, fishes, little frogs,
Invertebrates, aquatic slugs,
Crustaceans, microscopic bugs
And water plants. Perhaps you know
That anglers, not so long ago
In Britain, shot this treasured prize
For feathers to make fishing flies.
They stole its eggs and never paused
To think of all the harm they caused;
And so, by eighteen twenty-five
No Avocets were left alive.
Not 'til after World War Two
There came from Holland just a few
Intrepid Avocets, who thrived
Once conservationists arrived
And helped them and, I'm glad to say,
The Avocet's still here today.

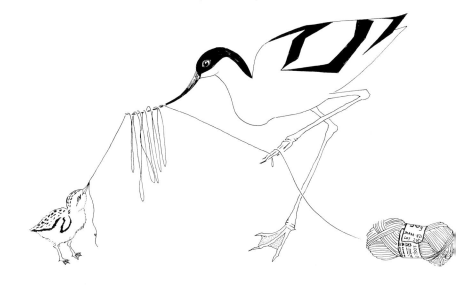

MEASUREMENTS

To fit bust: 81–86(91–97)cm
[32–34(36–38)in].
Actual measurement: 106(116)cm
[41¾(45¾)in].
Length from shoulder: approx
63(65)cm [24¾(25½)in].
Sleeve seam: 43(44)cm [17(17½)in].

MATERIALS

8(9) 50g balls of Avocet Chic in
cinnamon (912) – MC.
1 ball in each of yellow (916) – A;
cream (913) – E; oddment of black
(900) for embroidery.
1 50g ball of Avocet Soiree Chainette
in each of black (508) – B; white (504)
– C; blue (519) – D.
1 pair each of 3¼mm (US 3) and 4mm
(US 5) needles.
3¼mm (US 3) circular needle.
Spare needle.

TENSION

24sts and 30 rows to 10cm (4in) using
4mm (US 5) needles and st st using
MC.

FRONT

With 3¼mm (US 3) needles and MC,
cast on 107(117)sts and work in single
rib as follows:
1st row: (RS facing) K1, *P1, K1, rep
from * to end.
2nd row: P1, *K1, P1, rep from * to
end.
Rep these 2 rows until rib measures
8cm (3¼in), ending with a first row.
Increase row: Rib 4, M1, [rib 5, M1]
20(22) times, rib 3. [128(140)sts.]
Change to 4mm (US 5) needles and
starting with a K row, work 3 rows
straight in st st.
Joining in and breaking off colours as
required, cont in st st and colour patt
from chart, working between
appropriate lines for size required.
4th row: (WS facing) P13(19)MC, P4D,
P111(117)MC.
5th row: K112(118)MC, K4D,

K12(18)MC.
The chart is now placed.
Cont in patt from chart until 94 rows
of st st in all have been completed,
thus ending with a WS row.

Divide for front neck
Next row: Patt 60(66), K2tog, K2, turn
and leave rem sts on a spare needle
for right front, and cont on first set of
63(69)sts only for left front.
Work 1 row.

Shape armhole
Next row: (RS facing) Cast off 6(7)sts,
patt to last 4sts, K2tog, K2.
Work 1 row.
Next row: Patt to last 4sts, K2tog, K2.
Rep last 2 rows once more. Work 2
rows.
Next row: P2, P2tog, patt to end.
Work 2 rows.
Next row: Patt to last 4sts, K2tog, K2.
Work 2 rows.
Rep last 6 rows until 33(36)sts rem.
Work 2 rows after last dec. Cast off all
sts fairly loosely.
With RS facing rejoin MC to sts on
spare needle, K2, K2tog tbl, K to end.
[63(69)sts.]
Work 1 row.
Next row: K2, K2tog tbl, K to end.

Shape armhole
Cast off 6(7)sts at beg of next row, P to
end.
Next row: K2, K2tog tbl, K to end.
Work 1 row.
Next row: K2, K2tog tbl, K to end.
Work 2 rows.
Next row: P to last 4sts, P2tog tbl, P2.
Work 2 rows.
Rep last 6 rows until 33(36)sts rem.
Work 3 rows after last dec. Cast off all
sts fairly loosely.

BACK
Work as given for front, omitting
colour patt and neck shaping, until
back measures 6 rows less than on
front to cast-off shoulder edge, ending

with a WS row. [116(126)sts.]

Shape back neck
Next row: K48(51), and leave these sts
on a spare needle for right back, cast
off next 20(24)sts, K to end of row and
cont on this last set of 48(51)sts only
for left back.
Work 1 row.
** Cast off 5sts at beg (neck edge) on
next row and foll 2 alt rows.
Cast off rem 33(36)sts.
With WS facing rejoin MC to neck
edge of rem sts for right back and
work as given for left back to ** to
end.

SLEEVES (make 2)
With 3¼mm (US 3) needles and MC,
cast on 45(49)sts and work in single
rib as given for front welt for 3cm
(1¼in), ending with a 2nd row.
Break off MC, join in E.
Next row: K.
Cont in single rib as set until cuff
measures 6cm (2¼in), ending with a
first row.
Increase row: Rib 2, M1, [rib 3, M1, rib
2, M1] 8(9) times, rib 3(2). [62(68)sts.]
Break off E, join in MC.
Change to 4mm (US 5) needles and
starting with a K row work in st st, inc
1st at each end of 5th row and then
every foll 4th row until there are
112(122)sts on the needle.
Now work straight until sleeve
measures 43(44)cm [17(17½)in] from
cast-on edge.
Place a marker at each end of last row.
Work a further 2.5(3)cm [1(1¼)in] in
st st.
Cast off fairly loosely.

NECKBAND
Join both shoulder seams.
With the 3¼mm (US 3) circular
needle and MC and RS facing and beg
at centre of V, pick up and K67(72)sts
up right front to shoulder, 28(29)sts to
centre back neck, join in E and pick

up and K27(28)sts to left shoulder,
then 67(72)sts down left front to
centre of V. [189(201)sts.]
Starting with a 2nd row, work in **rows**
of single rib as for front welt, in
colours as set for 3cm (1¼in), taking
care to twist yarns when changing
colours to avoid a hole.
Cast off fairly loosely ribwise in
colours as set.

TO MAKE UP
Place right side of border over left
side at centre front and slip stitch ends
to pick-up row.
With centre of cast-off edges of sleeves
to shoulder seams, sew sleeves
carefully in position joining seam
above markers to cast-off sts at
underarm. Join side and sleeve seams.
Embroider eyes, using chain stitch
and French knots, as shown.

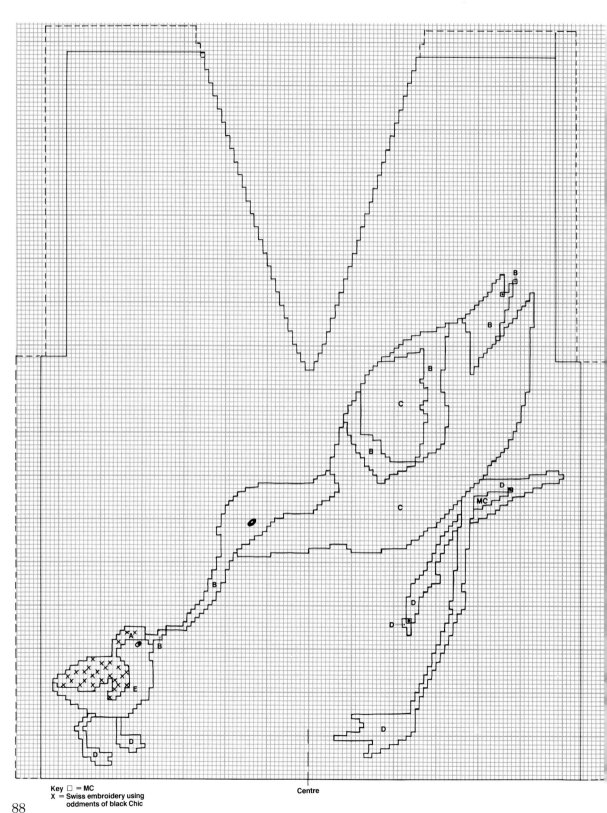

Key □ = MC
X = Swiss embroidery using
    oddments of black Chic

Centre

GRIFFON VULTURE
Gyps fulvus

Know ye the land where the cyprus and myrtle
Are emblems of deeds that are done in their clime?
Where the rage of the vulture, the love of the turtle,
Now melt into sorrow, now madden to crime!
            from *The Bride of Abydos* Lord Byron

Otherwise known as the Culture Vulture (*Cultura vulturus*) this bird is an extremely useful scavenger especially in local libraries, theatres, concert-halls, etc. It has no feathers on its head and neck because of its reading-habits, disliking the thought of fouling any feathers with dirty print as it forages amongst the pages of yesterday's newspaper. It will usually ignore prey that shows any signs of life and, in spite of its great size, refuses to get books off shelves for itself, preferring to rummage in waste-paper baskets for remaindered copies. Readers who have died of boredom are considered a particular delicacy. This helpful predator can save the overworked librarian much time spent tidying up.

The Culture Vulture usually nests on the ledges of theatre boxes. The single chick is fed on half-digested programmes and musical scores.

MEASUREMENTS

To fit bust: 81–86(91–97)cm
[32–34(36–38)in].
Actual measurement: 105(115)cm
[41½(45¼)in].
Length from shoulder: approx
63(65)cm [24¾(25½)in].
Sleeve seam: 43(44)cm [17(17½)in].

MATERIALS

11(13) 50g balls of 3-Suisses Caracus
in blue (00700) – MC.
1 50g ball of 3-Suisses Lorena in each
of mid-brown (05600) – A; light
brown (07800) – B; pale blue (02800)
– C.
1 50g ball of 3-Suisses Lanasport in
each of white (08000) – D; grey
(06800) – E; yellow (03700) – F.
1 50g ball of 3-Suisses Mohair 70 in
white (06000) – G.
1 reel of gold glitter sewing thread –
H.
1 pair each of 3¾mm (US 4) and
4½mm (US 6) needles.
3¾mm (US 4) circular needle.
Spare needle.
2 safety pins.

TENSION

19sts and 24 rows to 10cm (4in) using
4½mm (US 6) needles and st st using
MC.

NOTE

Yarns A and H are to be used together
throughout.

FRONT

With 3¾mm (US 4) needles and MC,
cast on 88(96)sts and work in K2, P2,
rib for 8cm (3¼in).
Increase row: Rib 6(3), M1, [rib 7, M1]
11(13) times, rib 5(2). [100(110)sts.]
Change to 4½mm (US 6) needles and
starting with a K row, work 4 rows
straight in st st.
Joining in and breaking off colours as
required, cont in st st and colour patt
from chart, working between
appropriate lines for size required.

5th row: (RS facing) K54(59)MC, K3E,
K43(48)MC.
6th row: P41(46)MC, P7E, P52(57)MC.
The chart is now placed.
Cont in patt from chart until 118(124)
rows of st st in all have been
completed, thus ending with a WS
row.

Shape front neck

Next row: K43(47), and leave these sts
on a spare needle for left front, cast off
next 14(16)sts, K to end of row and
cont on this last set of 43(47)sts only
for right front.
Work 1 row.
** **1st row:** Cast off 4sts (neck edge),
work to end.
2nd row: Cast off 11sts, work to end.
3rd row: As first row.
4th row: Cast off 10(12)sts, work to
end.
5th row: As first row.
Cast off rem 10(12)sts.
With WS facing rejoin MC to neck
edge of rem sts for left front and work
as given for right front from ** to end.

BACK

Work as given for front **BUT** after rib,
starting with a P row, work in reversed
st st, omitting colour patt and neck
shaping, until back measures the same
as front to beg of shoulder shaping,
ending with a WS row.

Shape shoulders

Cast off 11sts at beg of next 2 rows,
then 10(12)sts at beg of foll 4 rows.
Cast off rem 38(40)sts.

RIGHT SLEEVE AND SADDLE YOKE

With 3¾mm (US 4) needles and MC,
cast on 36(40)sts and work in K2, P2,
rib for 8cm (3¼in).
Increase row: Rib 5, M1, [rib 2, M1]
13(15) times, rib 5. [50(56)sts.]
Change to 4½mm (US 6) needles and
starting with a P row work in reversed
st st, inc 1st at each end of every foll
6th row until there are 56(60)sts on

the needle. Now inc 1st at each end of
every foll 4th row until there are
86(94)sts on the needle.
Work a few rows straight until sleeve
measures 43(44)cm [17(17½)in] from
cast-on edge, ending with a WS row.

Shape top

Cast off 24(26)sts at beg of next 2
rows. [38(42)sts.]
Work 1 row.
Dec 1st at each end of next row and
every foll 4th row until 20(22)sts
rem. ***
Work 2 rows, thus ending with a WS
row.

Shape neck

Cast off 5(6)sts at beg (front edge) of
next row, then dec 1st at same edge
on foll 3 rows.
Work a further 10(10.5)cm [4(4¼)in]
for back on rem 12(13)sts.
Leave sts on a safety-pin.

LEFT SLEEVE AND SADDLE YOKE

Work as for right sleeve to ***.
Work 1 row, thus ending with a RS
row.
Shape neck as given for right sleeve.

TO MAKE UP

Join saddle yoke at centre back by
grafting or casting off sts together.
Place a marker at each side of back
and front 12.5(13.5)cm [5(5½)in]
below shoulders. Join front above
markers to the 24(26) cast-off sts at
front edge of each sleeve, then join
shoulders to sloping edge of sleeve
extension. Join back to sleeves in
same way, then sew straight edge of
extension to cast-off sts at back neck.

NECKBAND

With the 3¾mm (US 4) circular
needle and MC and RS facing, start at
centre back and pick up and
K20(22)sts along straight edge,
10(11)sts along curved edge of yoke,
15sts down left front neck, 14(16)sts

across centre, 15sts up right front neck, 10(11)sts along curved edge of yoke, then 20(22)sts across back to centre. [104(112)sts.]
Work in **rounds** of K2, P2, rib for 6cm (2¼in).
Cast off fairly loosely ribwise.

TO COMPLETE
Fold neckband in half to inside and slip stitch loosely in position. Join side and sleeve seams. Embroider eye, using chain stitch and a French knot, as shown. Using a back stitch, embroider other features as shown.

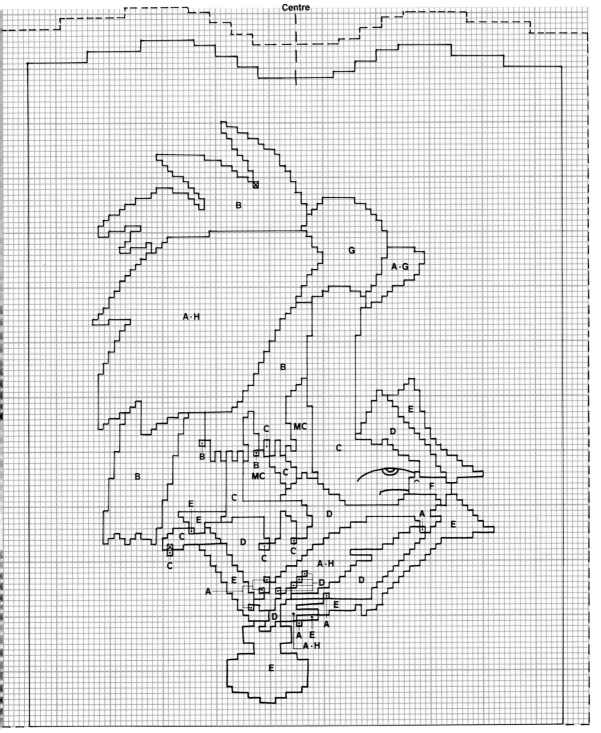

Centre

Key ⊠ = MC

SECRETARY BIRD
Sagittarius serpentarius

What . . .
Can't type
Can't read
Can't write
Can't spell
Can't tell the time
Can't answer the telephone
And still thinks it's a secretary . . .?

Answer: A bird

MEASUREMENTS

To fit bust: 81–86(91–97)cm [32–34(36–38)in].
Actual measurement: 105(114)cm [41¼(45)in].
Length from shoulder: approx 63(65)cm [24¾(25½)in].
Sleeve seam: 43(44)cm [17(17½)in].

MATERIALS

8(9) 50g balls of Pingouin Mohair in lilac (551) – MC.
1 ball in each of pink (512) – A; black (532) – B; grey (515) – C; oddments of yellow (542) – D; red (531) – E.
1 50g ball of Pingouin Fresque in white (01) – F.
1 pair each of 3¼mm (US 3) and 4mm (US 5) needles.
3¼mm (US 3) circular needle.
Spare needle.

TENSION

22sts and 31 rows to 10cm (4in) using 4mm (US 5) needles and st st using MC.

SPECIAL ABBREVIATION FOR THIS PATTERN

SKTPO = slip next 2sts together (as if to K2tog), K1, then pass the 2 slipped sts over.

FRONT

With 3¼mm (US 3) needles and MC, cast on 101(109)sts and work in single rib as follows:
1st row: (RS facing) K1, *P1, K1, rep from * to end.
2nd row: P1, *K1, P1, rep from * to end.
Rep these 2 rows until rib measures 8cm (3¼in), ending with a first row.
Increase row: Rib 8(6), M1, [rib 6, M1] 14(16) times, rib 9(7). [116(126)sts.]
Change to 4mm (US 5) needles and starting with a K row, work 5 rows straight in st st.
Joining in and breaking off colours as required, cont in st st and colour patt from chart, working between

appropriate lines for size required.
6th row: (WS facing) P46(51)MC, P1A, P69(74)MC.
7th row: K70(75)MC, K1A, K45(50)MC.
The chart is now placed.
Cont in patt from chart until 90 rows of st st in all have been completed, thus ending with a WS row.

Shape armholes

Keeping patt correct, cast off 3sts at beg of next 2 rows.
Dec 1st at each end of next 3(5) rows, then on foll 2 alt rows. [100(106)sts.]
Work straight until 154(160) rows of st st in all have been completed, thus ending with a WS row.

Shape front neck

Next row: K43(45), and leave these sts on a spare needle for left front, cast off next 14(16)sts, K to end of row and cont on this last set of 43(45)sts only for right front.
Work 1 row.
** Cast off 4sts at beg (neck edge) of next row, then 3sts at beg of foll alt row.
Dec 1st at neck edge on next 9 rows, then on foll alt row.
Work 1 row. Cast off rem 26(28)sts.
With WS facing rejoin MC to neck edge of rem sts for left front and work as for right front from ** to end.

BACK

Work as given for front, omitting colour patt and neck shaping, until 8 rows less than on front have been worked to cast-off shoulder edge, ending with a WS row.

Shape back neck

Next row: K42(44), and leave these sts on a spare needle for right back, cast off next 16(18)sts, K to end of row and cont on this last set of 42(44)sts only for left back.
Work 1 row.

*** Cast off 4sts at beg (neck edge) on next row and foll 3 alt rows.
Cast off rem 26(28)sts.
With WS facing rejoin MC to neck edge of rem sts for right back and work as for left back from *** to end.

SLEEVES (make 2)

With 3¼mm (US 3) needles and MC, cast on 45(49)sts and work in single rib as given for front welt for 6cm (2¼in), ending with a first row.
Increase row: Rib 3(5), M1, [rib 1, M1, rib 2, M1] 13 times, rib 3(5). [72(76)sts.]
Change to 4mm (US 5) needles and starting with a K row work in st st, inc 1st at each end of 5th row and then every foll 5th row until there are 114(122)sts on the needle.
Now work straight until sleeve measures 43(44)cm [17(17½)in] from cast-on edge, ending with a WS row.

Shape top

Cast off 4sts at beg of next 14(16) rows, 5sts at beg of next 2 rows, 6sts at beg of foll 2 rows, then 7sts at beg of next 2 rows.
Cast off rem 22sts fairly loosely.

NECKBAND

Join both shoulder seams.
With the 3¼mm (US 3) circular needle, MC and RS facing and starting at centre back, pick up and K30(32)sts to left shoulder, 1st at shoulder (mark this st), 71(75)sts around front neck, 1st at right shoulder (mark this st), then 31(33)sts around to centre back. [134(142)sts.]
Work in **rounds** of K1, P1, rib for 2 rounds.

Shape sides of shoulders

3rd round: Rib to within 1st of marked st, SKTPO, rib to within 1st of 2nd marked st, SKTPO, rib to end. Cont to dec at each side

of shoulder on every foll 4th round
until neckband measures
6cm (2¼in). Cast off fairly loosely
ribwise.

TO MAKE UP

Join side and sleeve seams. With
centre of cast-off edges of sleeves to
shoulder seams, sew sleeves carefully
into armholes. Embroider eye, using
chain stitch and a French knot, as
shown.

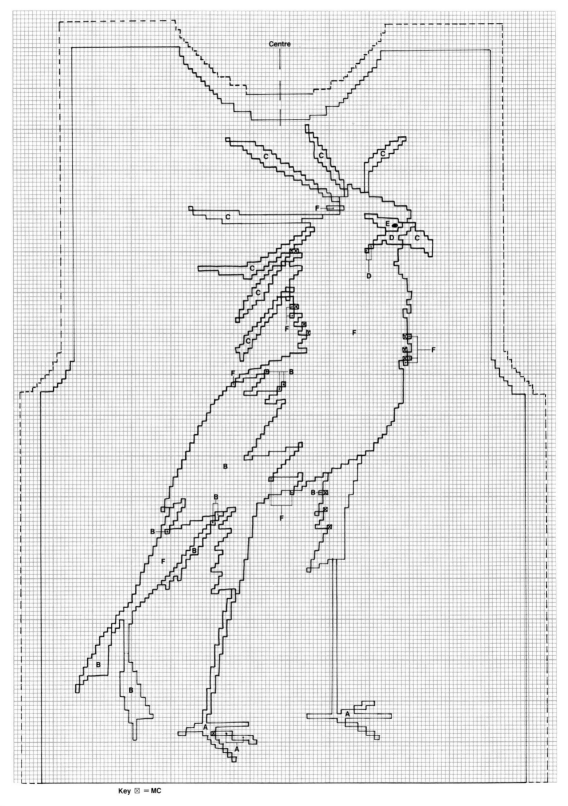

Centre

Key ⊠ = MC

DODO

Raphus cucullatus

'But who has won?'
This question the Dodo could not answer without a great deal
of thought, and it stood for a long time with one finger
pressed upon its forehead (the position in which you usually
see Shakespeare, in the pictures of him), while the rest waited
in silence. At last the Dodo said, '*Everybody* has won, and *all*
must have prizes.'

Alice's Adventures in Wonderland Lewis Carroll

Dodos never have had much luck, really. They are supposed to
have been discovered by Dutch sailors in the sixteenth century
on the islands of Mauritius, Reunion and Rodriguez. Each island
had its own species of Dodo. The Mauritius lot were extinct by
1700, in Reunion they had disappeared by the 1750s and on
Rodriguez they lasted until about 1800. They seem to have been
killed off by pigs and monkeys introduced into the islands by the
Portuguese. The Dutch thought the Dodo had a 'stupid and
voracious physiognomy' and called it 'the nauseous bird, as well
from its disgusting figure as from the bad taste of its flesh'. The
Portuguese pigs and monkeys appear to have been less
particular.

MEASUREMENTS

To fit bust: 81–86(91–97)cm [32–34(36–38)in].

Actual measurement: 103(113)cm [40½(44½)in].

Length from shoulder: approx 60(63)cm [23½(24¾in)].

Sleeve seam: approx 45cm [17¾in].

MATERIALS

8(9) 50g balls of Tootal Craft Legend in fuchsia (712) – MC.

1 ball in each of grey (709) – A; white (700) – B; black (714) – E.

1 50g ball of Tootal Craft Tapestry in each of Sampler (730) – C; Raphael (732) – D.

1 pair each of 6mm (US 9) and 7½mm (US 11) needles.

Spare needle.

TENSION

12sts and 15 rows to 10cm (4in) using 7½mm (US 11) needles and st st using MC.

SPECIAL ABBREVIATION FOR THIS PATTERN

ML = insert needle into next st as if to K, wrap yarn over needle and forefinger 3 times, then over needle again and draw yarn through st (there are now 4 loops on right-hand needle), insert left needle into front of these 4 loops and K4tog from this position.

PATTERN FOR TAIL OF DODO

(marked BX on chart – worked in B).

1st and 3rd rows: (RS facing) K.

2nd row: *M1, K1, rep from * to end.

4th row: *K1, ML, rep from * to end.

These 4 rows form the BX pattern and are repeated as required, working it into chart and correcting number of sts as necessary to keep chart correct.

NOTE

When changing quality (from Legend to Tapestry or vice-versa), always work first row K on right side and P on wrong side.

FRONT

With 6mm (US 9) needles and MC, cast on 58(62)sts and work in K1, P1, rib for 6cm (2¼in).

Increase row: Rib 8(6), M1, [rib 14(10), M1] 3(5) times, rib 8(6). [62(68)sts.]

Change to 7½mm (US 11) needles and starting with a K row, work 7 rows straight in st st.

Joining in and breaking off colours as required, cont in st st and colour patt from chart, working between appropriate lines for size required.

8th row: (WS facing) P29(32)MC, P1A, P32(35)MC.

9th row: K29(32)MC, K1A, K3MC, K1A, K28(31)MC.

The chart is now placed.

Cont in patt from chart, working in reversed st st and BX pattern as indicated, until 42 rows of st st in all have been completed, thus ending with a WS row.

Shape armholes

Keeping patt correct, cast off 3(4)sts at beg of next 2 rows. [56(60)sts.]

Cont straight until 72(76)rows of st st in all have been completed, thus ending with a WS row.

Shape front neck

Next row: K23(24), and leave these sts on a spare needle for left front, cast off next 10(12)sts, K to end of row and cont on this last set of 23(24)sts only for right front.

Work 1 row.

** Dec 1st at neck edge on next 5 rows, then at same edge on foll alt row.

Cast off rem 17(18)sts.

With WS facing rejoin MC to neck edge of rem sts for left front and work as for right front from ** to end.

BACK

Work in st st as given for front, omitting colour patt and neck

shaping, until 4 rows less than on front have been worked to cast-off shoulder edge, ending with a WS row.

Shape back neck

Next row: K23(24), and leave these sts on a spare needle for right back, cast off next 10(12)sts, K to end of row and cont on this last set of 23(24)sts only for left back.

Work 1 row.

*** Cast off 6sts at beg (neck edge) of next row.

Work 2 rows.

Cast off rem 17(18)sts.

With WS facing rejoin MC to neck edge of rem sts for right back and work as for left back from *** to end.

SLEEVES (make 2)

With 6mm (US 9) needles and MC, cast on 32(34)sts and work in K1, P1, rib for 4cm (1¾in).

Increase row: Rib 2(3), M1, [rib 4, M1] 7 times, rib 2(3). [40(42)sts.]

Change to 7½mm (US 11) needles and starting with a K row work in st st, inc 1st at each end of 5th row and then every foll 6th row until there are 58(56)sts on the needle. Now inc 1st at each end of every foll 4th row until there are 62(68)sts on the needle.

Work a few rows straight until sleeve measures 47(48)cm [18½(19)in] from cast-on edge, ending with a WS row.

Cast off all sts fairly loosely.

NECKBAND

Join right shoulder seam.

With 6mm (US 9) needles and MC, RS facing, pick up and K34(38)sts evenly around front neck and 30(32)sts evenly around back neck. [64(70)sts.]

Work in K1, P1, rib for 6cm (2¼in).

Cast off fairly loosely ribwise.

TO MAKE UP

Join left shoulder seam and neckband. Fold neckband in half to inside and slip stitch loosely in position. With

centre of cast-off edges of sleeves to shoulder seams, sew sleeves carefully in position, joining top of sleeve seam to cast-off sts at underarm. Join side and sleeve seams. Embroider eye, using chain stitch and a French knot.

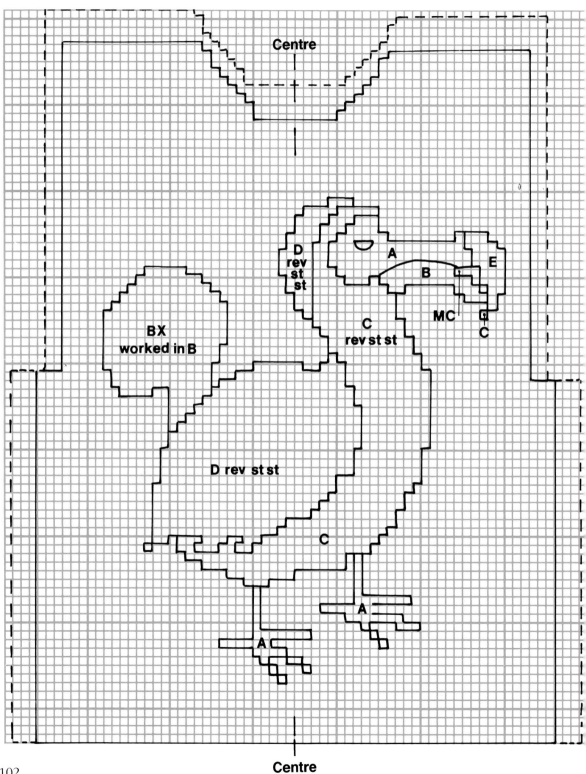

CANARIES
Serinus canaria

Mary had a pretty bird
Feathers bright and yellow
Slender legs, upon my word
He was a pretty fellow.
The sweetest notes he always sang
Which much delighted Mary
And near the cage she'd ever sit
To hear her own canary
          Traditional nursery-rhyme

Mary is supposed to have been Mary, Queen of Scots and her
'pretty bird' David Rizzio, her Italian secretary, who serenaded
her with passionate songs. He came to a very sticky end, stabbed
forty times by the jealous Lord Darnley and Lord Ruthven, and
was buried at the foot of the stairs leading to Mary's apartments.

Canaries are a variety of finch, otherwise known as siskins.
They still exist in the wild on the Canary Islands, the Azores and
on Madeira. They were brought to Germany in the sixteenth
century where they were domesticated and exported all over
Europe.

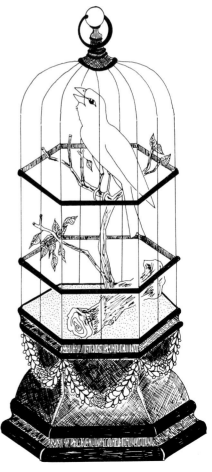

MEASUREMENTS

To fit bust: 81–86(91–97)cm
32–34(36–38)in].
Actual measurement: 101(111)cm
39¾(43¾)in].
Length from shoulder: approx
60(62)cm [23½(24½)in].
Sleeve seam: 23(25)cm [9(9¾)in].

MATERIALS

7(9) 50g balls of Scheepjeswol Linnen
in white (261) – MC.
1 ball in each of grey (254) – A; green
(253) – B; pale yellow (272) –C;
mid-yellow (271) – D.
1 pair each of 3mm (US 2) and 3¾mm
(US 4) needles.
3mm (US 2) circular needle.
3 buttons.
Spare needle.

TENSION

24sts and 32 rows to 10cm (4in) using
3¾mm (US 4) needles and st st using
MC.

FRONT

With 3mm (US 2) needles and MC,
cast on 101(109)sts and work in single
rib as follows:
1st row: (RS facing) K1, *P1, K1, rep
from * to end.
2nd row: P1, *K1, P1, rep from * to
end.
Rep these 2 rows until rib measures
8cm (3¼in), ending with a first row.
Increase row: Rib 6, M1, [rib 5(4), M1,
rib 4, M1] 10(12) times, rib 5(7).
[122(134)sts.]
Change to 3¾mm (US 4) needles and
starting with a K row, work 71 rows
straight in st st.
Joining in and breaking off colours as
required, cont in st st and colour patt
from chart, working between
appropriate lines for size required.
72nd row: (WS facing) P34(40)MC,
P1D, P59MC, P2C, P26(32)MC.
73rd row: K26(32)MC, K2C, K53MC,
K1D, K4MC, K2D, K34(40)MC.

The chart is now placed.
Cont in patt from chart until 90 rows
of st st in all have been completed,
thus ending with a WS row.

Shape armholes

Keeping patt correct, cast off 3(4)sts at
beg of next 2 rows.
Dec 1st at each end of next 5(7) rows,
then on foll 2 alt rows. [102(108)sts.]
Work straight until 135(141) rows of st
st in all have been completed, thus
ending with a RS row.

Divide for front opening

Next row: P48(51), and leave these sts
on a spare needle for right front, cast
off next 6sts, P to end of row and cont
on this last set of 48(51)sts only for left
front.
** Work 11 rows straight.

Shape neck

Dec 1st at neck edge on next 8(10)
rows.
Cast off 3sts at beg (neck edge) of next
row and foll 5 alt rows.
Cast off rem 22(23)sts.
With RS facing rejoin MC to neck edge
of rem 48(51)sts for right front and
work as given for left front from ** to
end, but work 1 extra row before
working 'cast off 3sts' to keep shaping
at beg of RS rows.

BACK

Work as given for front, omitting
colour patt and neck shaping, until
back measures 4 rows less than on
front to cast-off shoulder edge, ending
with a WS row.

Shape back neck

Next row: K36(39), and leave these sts
on a spare needle for right back, cast
off next 30sts, K to end of row and
cont on this last set of 36(39)sts only
for left back.
Work 1 row.
*** Cast off 7(8)sts at beg (neck edge)
of next and foll alt row.

Cast off rem 22(23)sts.
With WS facing rejoin MC to neck
edge of rem sts for right back and
work as given for left back from *** to
end.

SLEEVES (make 2)

With 3mm (US 2) needles and MC,
cast on 75(81)sts and starting with a K
row work 2 rows in st st.
Change to 3¾mm (US 4) needles and
cont in st st, inc 1st at each end of next
row and then every foll 3rd row until
there are 115(127)sts on the needle.
Work a few rows straight until sleeve
measures 20(22)cm [8(8½)in] from
cast-on edge, ending with a WS row.

Shape top

Cast off 3sts at beg of next 8 rows,
4(5)sts at beg of foll 12 rows, 5sts at
beg of next 2 rows then 6sts at beg of
foll 2 rows.
Cast off rem 21sts fairly loosely.

NECKBAND

Join both shoulder seams.
With the 3mm (US 2) circular needle,
MC and RS facing and beg at base of
front opening, pick up and K10sts up
right side of opening, 35(36)sts up
right front to shoulder, 67(71)sts
around back neck, 35(36)sts down left
front, then 10sts down left side of
front opening. [157(163)sts.]
Starting with a 2nd row work 3 **rows**
in single rib as given for front welt.
Buttonhole row: (RS facing) Rib 6,
cast off 3sts, rib to end.
Next row: Rib, casting on 3sts over
cast-off sts on previous row.
Rib 2 more rows.
Cast off fairly loosely ribwise.

ARMBANDS (make 2)

With 3mm (US 2) needles and MC,
cast on 11sts and work in rib as
follows:
1st row: (RS facing) K2, [P1, K1] 4
times, K1.
2nd row: P2, [K1, P1] 4 times, P1.

Rep these 2 rows until band measures 32(34)cm [12½(13½)in] from cast-on edge, ending with a 2nd row.

Shape end
Cast off 1st at each end of next 4 rows. Cast off rem 3sts.

TO MAKE UP
Join side and sleeve seams. With centre of cast-off edges of sleeves to shoulder seams, sew sleeves carefully into armholes. Lay right side of neckband over left and stitch neatly together at base of opening.
Sew armbands to lower edges of sleeves as in photo, easing sleeve to fit and overlapping pointed end of band 2cm (¾in). Sew on 1 button to each armband working through two thicknesses. Sew button to neck border to correspond with buttonhole. Embroider eyes, using chain stitch and French knots, as shown. Using chain stitch, embroider legs and feet.

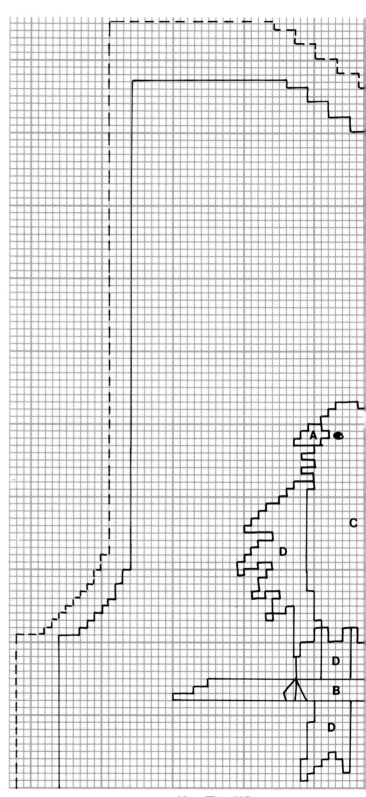

Key ☒ = **MC**

Centre

A

A

C

C

D

D

B

C

B

GREAT SPOTTED WOODPECKER

Dendrocopus major

> . . . With shrill and oft-repeated cry,
> Her angular course, alternate rise and fall,
> The woodpecker prolongs; then to the trunk
> Close clinging, with unwearied beak assails
> The hollow bark; through every cell the strokes
> Roll the dire echoes that from wintry sleep
> Awake her insect prey; . . .
>
> from *Walks in a Forest* Thomas Gisborne

The Woodpecker's song is supposed to be a call for rain because God condemned them to drinking nothing but rainwater for refusing to help all the other birds to make the rivers, ponds and oceans in the Creation.

In Sweden they have a variation on the Owl fable (see the Great Horned Owl introduction); they call the Woodpecker 'Gertrude's Fowl' because they believe that an old woman called Gertrude refused to give bread to Christ and to St Peter and was turned into a Woodpecker, condemned to drinking rainwater for the rest of her days.

Don't knit this sweater for anyone who keeps bees. Bee-keepers aren't mad keen on Woodpeckers because they sometimes raid hives in search of a change of diet.

109

MEASUREMENTS

To fit bust: 81–86(91–97)cm [32–34(36–38)in].

Width from centre back to cuff: approx 59(62)cm [23½(24½)in].

Length from shoulder: approx 61(63)cm [24(24¾)in].

MATERIALS

12(14) 50g balls of Wendy Fiori in pale yellow (569) – MC.

1 50g ball of Wendy Family Choice Chunky in each of black (530) – A; white (510) – B; red (527) – C; beige (516) – D.

1 50g ball of Wendy Video in black/white speckled (188) – E.

1 pair each of 4½mm (US 6) and 5½mm (US 8) needles.

5½mm (US 8) circular needle.

Cable needle.

Spare needle.

TENSION

16sts and 22 rows to 10cm (4in) using 5½mm (US 8) needles and st st using MC.

CABLE PANEL (worked over 6sts)

1st, 3rd and 7th rows: (RS facing) K6.

2nd and every alt row: P6.

5th row: Slip first 4sts on to cable needle and hold at front of work, K2, then K4 from cable needle.

8th row: As 2nd row.

These 8 rows form the cable panel and are repeated as required.

FRONT

With 4½mm (US 6) needles and MC, cast on 72(80)sts and work in K2, P2, rib for 10cm (4in).

Increase row: [Rib 6, M1] 3 times, [rib 8(9), M1] 6 times, rib 6(8). [81(89)sts.] Change to 5½mm (US 8) needles and work in patt as follows:

1st row: (RS facing) K59(63), P2, [work across first row of cable panel, P4(5)] twice, K0(2).

2nd row: P0(2), [K4(5), work across 2nd row of cable panel] twice, K2,

P59(63).

Cont in st st and cable panels as set, repeating the 8 rows as required, **at the same time**, shape sides as follows, changing to the 5½mm (US 8) circular needle when necessary, and cont to work in **rows**:

at right side of work, inc 1st on 7th row and then every foll 4th row 6 times, then foll 11 alt rows,

at left side of work, inc 1st on 5th row then [foll 3rd and foll 4th row, thus inc 2sts every 7 rows] 4 times, foll 9 alt rows, then on next 3 rows, work inc sts into cable patt. [120(128)sts.]

With RS facing, cast on 4sts at beg of next 3 rows, 5sts at beg of foll 4 rows, then *at left side of work* cast on 6(7)sts, then 7sts on foll alt row, work inc sts into cable patt,

at right side of work cast on 5sts. [170(179)sts.]

At the same time, when 5 rows of st st in all have been completed, joining in and breaking off colours as required, cont in st st and colour patt from chart, working between appropriate lines for size required.

6th row: (WS facing) Patt 57(61)MC, P1A, P24(28)MC.

7th row: Inc in first st, K24(28)MC, K1A, patt 56(60)MC.

The chart is now placed.

Cont in patt from chart, working incs as given, and then working straight in st st and cable panels until 98(102) rows of st st in all have been completed, thus ending with a WS row.

Shape front neck

Next row: K71(74), and leave these sts on a spare needle for left front, cast off next 18(20)sts, patt to end of row and cont on this last set of 81(85)sts only for right front.

Dec 1st at neck edge on next 6 rows, then at same edge on foll alt row, thus ending at sleeve edge.

Shape shoulder

1st row: (WS facing) Cast off 17(18)sts, patt to end.

2nd row: K2tog, patt to end.

3rd row: As first row.

4th row: In patt.

Cast off rem 39(41)sts.

With WS facing rejoin MC to neck edge of rem sts for left front, P2tog, P to end of row.

Dec 1st at same edge on next 5 rows. Work 1 row, thus ending at sleeve edge.

Shape shoulder

1st row: Cast off 15(16)sts, K to last 2sts, K2tog.

2nd row: P.

Rep first and 2nd rows.

Cast off rem 33(34)sts.

BACK

With 4½mm (US 6) needles and MC, cast on 72(80)sts and work in K2, P2, rib for 10cm (4in).

Increase row: Rib 6(8), [M1, rib 8(9)] 6 times, [M1, rib 6] 3 times. [81(89)sts.] Change to 5½mm (US 8) needles and work in patt as follows:

1st row: (RS facing) K0(2), [P4(5), work across first row of cable panel] twice, P2, K59(63).

2nd row: P59(63), K2, [work across 2nd row of cable panel, K4(5)] twice, P0(2).

Cont in st st and cable panels as set, **at the same time**, shape sides by reversing incs as given for front, taking inc sts at right side into cable panel and omitting colour patt and neck shaping.

Cont in st st and cable panels, until 1 row less than on front has been worked to beg of shoulder shaping, ending with a RS row.

Shape back neck

Next row: P73(76), and leave these sts on a spare needle for left back, cast off next 14(16)sts, patt to end of row and cont on this last set of 83(87)sts only for right back.

1st row: Cast off 17(18)sts, patt to end.

2nd row: Cast off 5sts, patt to end.

Rep first and 2nd rows.

Cast off rem 39(41)sts.

With RS facing, rejoin MC to neck edge of rem sts for left back and K to end.

1st row: Cast off 15(16)sts, P to end.

2nd row: Cast off 5sts, K to end.

Rep these 2 rows.

Cast off rem 33(34)sts.

NECKBAND

Join right shoulder seam, matching patts.

With 4½mm (US 6) needles and MC and RS facing, pick up and K48(52)sts around front neck, then 40(44)sts around back neck. [88(96)sts.]

Work in K2, P2, rib for 2cm (¾in).

Cast off fairly loosely ribwise.

CUFFS (alike)

Join left shoulder seam and neckband.

With 4½mm (US 6) needles and MC and RS facing, pick up and K36(40)sts evenly along lower edge of one sleeve.

Work in K2, P2, rib for 6cm (2¼in).

Cast off fairly loosely ribwise.

TO COMPLETE

Join side and underarm seams.

Embroider eye and claws, using chain stitch, as shown.

As this yarn knits up loosely, it may be necessary to add a few rows of shirring elastic to cuffs, neckband and welt to keep elasticity.

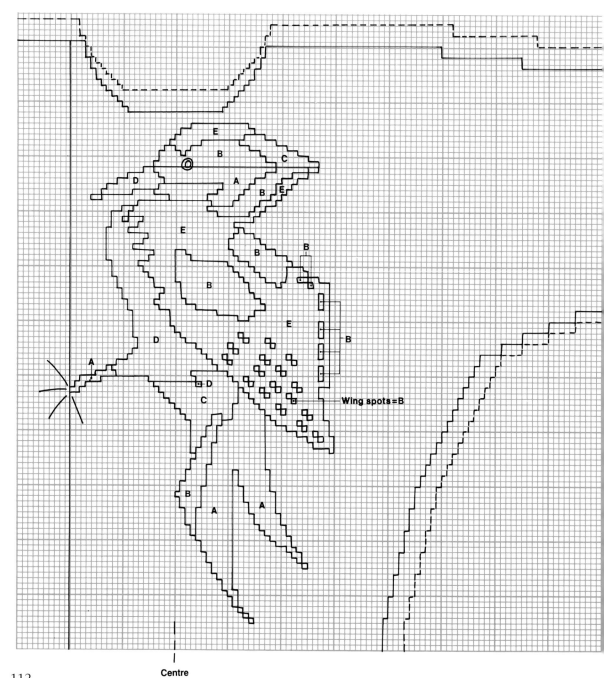

Centre

BUDGERIGARS
Melopsittacus undulatus

Miss Ward to the Budgerigar:

Dear Budgie, in your gilded cage,
Believe me, this advice is sage:
Because you are a household pet
Your perch is by the TV set.
Please note with your observant eye
A yellow bird called Tweetie-pie.
Do not, I beg you, emulate
The cuteness that has made her great.
Although the bird could not be sweeter
The cat, I hope, will one day eat her.

Lord Birkett

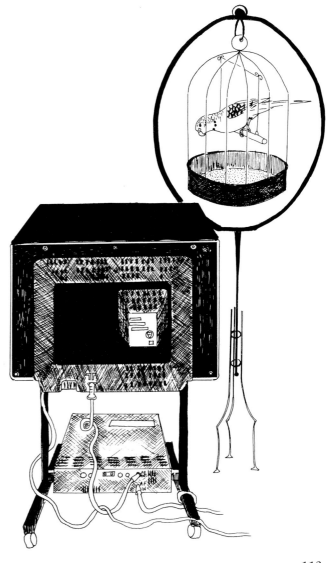

MEASUREMENTS

To fit bust: 81–86(91–97)cm
[32–34(36–38)in].
Actual measurement: 105(115)cm
[41¼(45¼)in].
Length from shoulder: approx
57(58)cm [22½(23)in].
Sleeve seam: approx 35cm (13¾in).

MATERIALS

11(13) 50g balls of Twilleys Stalite in
white (78) – MC.
1 ball in yellow (68) – A.
1 50g ball of Twilleys Perlespun in
each of blue (128) – B; green (181) –
C; beige (106) – D; black (179) – F.
2 balls in grey (115) – E.
1 pair each of 2¾mm (US 1) and
3¼mm (US 3) needles.
Spare needle.

TENSION

28sts and 38 rows to 10cm (4in) using
3¼mm (US 3) needles and st st using
MC.

SPECIAL ABBREVIATIONS FOR THIS PATTERN

sl3P = slip 3sts purlways.
sl2P = slip 2sts purlways.
yft = with yarn to front of work.
yb = take yarn to back of work.

NOTE

When working sl3P on 'perch' patt,
hold yarn LOOSELY on right side of
work.

FRONT

With 2¾mm (US 1) needles and MC
cast on 120(128)sts and work in K2,
P2, rib for 4cm (1¾in).
Increase row: Rib 8, M1, [rib 4, M1, rib
4(3), M1] 13(16) times, rib 8.
[147(161)sts.]
Change to 3¼mm (US 3) needles and
starting with a K row, work 64 rows
straight in st st.
Joining in and breaking off colours as
required, cont in st st and colour patt
from chart, working between

appropriate lines for size required.
65th row: (RS facing) K42(49)MC,
K1B, K104(111)MC.
66th row: P104(111)MC, P1B,
P42(49)MC.
The chart is now placed.
Cont in patt from chart until 99 rows
of st st in all have been completed,
thus ending with a RS row.
Break MC, join in D and work in perch
patt as follows:
1st row: (WS facing) P.
2nd and 4th rows: K2(1), *yft, sl3P, yb,
K1, rep from * to last 1(0)st, K1(0).
3rd row: P2(1), *yb, sl3P, yft, K1, rep
from * to last 1(0)st, P1(0).
5th row: P.
6th and 8th rows: [K1, yft, sl2P, yb]
1(0) time, K1(3), *yft, sl3P, yb, K1, rep
from * to last 3(2)sts, [yft, sl2P, yb] 1(0)
time, K1(2).
7th row: [P1, yb, sl2P, yft] 1(0) time,
P1(3), *yb, sl3P, yft, P1, rep from * to
last 3(2)sts, [yb, sl2P, yft] 1(0) time,
P1(2).
9th to 12th rows: Rep 1st to 4th rows.
Break D, rejoin MC and work 5 rows
in colour patt from chart, thus ending
with a WS row.

Shape armholes

Keeping patt correct, cast off 5(6)sts at
beg of next 2 rows.
Dec 1st at each end of next 5(7) rows,
then on foll 3 alt rows. [121(129)sts.]
Now cont straight in patt until 78(82)
rows of st st in all have been worked
from beg of armhole shaping, thus
ending with a WS row.

Shape front neck

Next row: K49(51), and leave these sts
on a spare needle for left front, cast off
next 23(27)sts, K to end of row, and
cont on this last set of 49(51)sts only
for right front.
Work 1 row.
** Cast off 5sts at beg (neck edge) of
next row and foll 3 alt rows.
Dec 1st at same edge on next 5 rows,

then on foll alt row.
Work 1 row. Cast off rem 23(25)sts.
With WS facing rejoin MC to neck
edge of rem sts for left front and work
as given for right front from ** to end.

BACK

Work as given for front, omitting
colour patt and stitch patt (perch)
until back measures the same as front
to beg of armhole shaping, ending
with a WS row.
Complete as given for front.

LEFT SLEEVE

With 2¾mm (US 1) needles and MC,
cast on 60(64)sts and work in K2, P2,
rib for 4cm (1¾in).
Increase row: Rib 5(7), M1, [rib 2, M1]
25 times, rib 5(7). [86(90)sts.]
Change to 3¼mm (US 3) needles, join
in E and starting with a K row work in
st st and stripe patt as follows:
Work 12 rows E, 2 rows B, 12 rows
MC.
These 26 rows form the stripe patt and
are repeated as required, **at the same
time,** inc 1st at each end of 3rd row
and then every foll 4th row until there
are 138(144)sts on the needle.
Work a few rows straight until sleeve
measures approx 35cm (13¾in) from
cast-on edge, ending with a 6th row of
stripe patt in E.

Shape top

Keeping stripe patt correct, cast off
5(6)sts at beg of next 6 rows, then 5sts
at beg of foll 14 rows.
Cast off rem 38sts.

RIGHT SLEEVE

Work as given for left sleeve, but use C
in place of B in stripe patt.

NECKBAND

Join right shoulder seam.
With 2¾mm (US 1) needles and MC
and RS facing, pick up and K30sts
down left front neck, 26(30)sts across
centre front, 30sts up right front neck,

then pick up sts for back neck in the
same way. [172(180)sts.]
Work in K2, P2, rib for 5 rows.
Shape as follows:
1st row: (RS facing) Rib 166(174),
turn.
2nd row: Sl 1, rib 159(167), turn.
3rd row: Sl 1, rib 153(161), turn.
Cont in this way working 6sts fewer at
end of every row until the row 'sl 1,
rib 51(59), turn' has been worked.
Next row: Sl 1, rib to end.
Now work 3 rows in rib across all sts.
Cast off fairly loosely ribwise.

TO MAKE UP

Join left shoulder seam and neckband.
Fold neckband in half to inside and
slip stitch loosely in position. Join side
and sleeve seams matching stripes.
With centre of cast-off edges of sleeves
to shoulder seams sew sleeves
carefully into armholes.
Embroider eyes, using chain stitch
and French knots, as shown. With a
back stitch, embroider claws. Work
markings on head and back of birds in
Swiss embroidery using F.

Note: 'spots' on head and back
are Swiss-embroidered with F
on completion of garment.

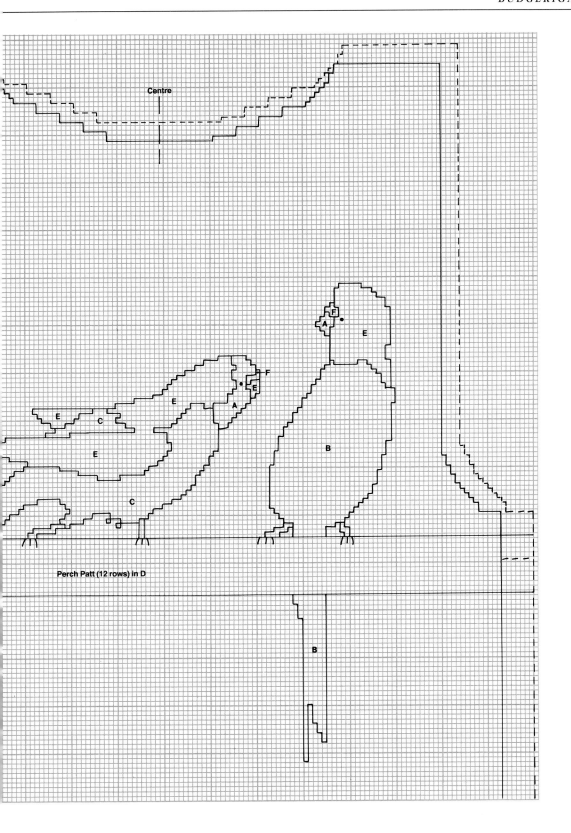

Centre

F
A
E

F
E
A
E
E
C
E
E
C
B

B

Perch Patt (12 rows) in D

B

GENTOO PENGUINS
Pygoscelis papua

You'll only find the Penguin
In the Southern Hemisphere:
For fifty million years or so
The Penguin has lived there.
Although these birds are clumsy
And ungainly on dry land,
In water they make up for it,
Or so I understand.
At twenty miles an hour or more
They'll beat the Leopard Seal
And just as well unless they want
To end up as a meal.

MEASUREMENTS

To fit bust: 81–86(91–97)cm
[32–34(36–38)in].
Actual measurement: 104(113)cm
[41(44½)in].
Length from shoulder: approx
64(65)cm [25¼(25½)in].
Sleeve seam: approx 44(45)cm
[17½(17¾)in].

MATERIALS

7(8) 50g balls of Pingouin Pingofrance
in pale blue (103) – MC.
4(5) balls in white (101) – A.
1 50g ball of Pingouin Rubane in each
of white (10) – B; grey (18) – C; black
(17) – D; yellow (04) – E.
1 pair each of 3¼mm (US 3) and 4mm
(US 5) needles.
3¼mm (US 3) and 4mm (US 5)
circular needles.
Spare needle.

TENSION

23sts and 30 rows to 10cm (4in) using
4mm (US 5) needles and st st using
MC.

FRONT

With 3¼mm (US 3) needles and MC,
cast on 100(108)sts and work in K2,
P2, rib for 8cm (3¼in).
Increase row: Rib 2, M1, [rib 5, M1]
19(21) times, rib 3(1). [120(130)sts.]
Change to 4mm (US 5) needles and
starting with a K row, work 10 rows
straight in st st.
Joining in and breaking off colours as
required, cont in st st and colour patt
from chart, working between
appropriate lines for size required.
11th row: (RS facing) K93(98)MC,
K1E, K26(31)MC.
12th row: P25(30)MC, P2E,
P93(98)MC.
The chart is now placed.
Cont in patt from chart until 90 rows
of st st in all have been completed,
thus ending with a WS row.

Shape armholes

Keeping patt correct, cast off 8(10)sts
at beg of next 2 rows. [104(110)sts.]
Work straight in patt until 154(158)
rows of st st in all have been
completed, thus ending with a WS
row.

Shape front neck

Next row: K45(47), and leave these sts
on a spare needle for left front, cast off
next 14(16)sts, K to end of row and
cont on this last set of 45(47)sts only
for right front.
Work 1 row.
** Cast off 5sts at beg (neck edge) of
next row.
Dec 1st at same edge on next 9 rows,
then on foll alt row. [30(32)sts.]
Work 1 row.
Cast off all sts.
With WS facing rejoin A to neck edge
of rem sts for left front and work as
given for right front from ** to end.

BACK

Work as given for front, omitting
colour patt, until 5 rows less than on
front to armhole have been worked,
thus ending with a RS row.
Break off MC and join in A.
Cont in A only and work 5 rows, thus
ending with a WS row.

Shape armholes

Cast off 8(10)sts at beg of next 2 rows.
[104(110)sts.]
Work straight in st st until 6 rows less
than on back have been worked to
cast-off shoulder edge, ending with a
WS row.

Shape back neck

Next row: K42(44)sts and leave these
sts on a spare needle for right back,
cast off next 20(22)sts, K to end of row
and cont on this last set of 42(44)sts
only for left back.
Work 1 row.
*** Cast off 4sts at beg (neck edge) of
next row and foll 2 alt rows.

Cast off rem 30(32)sts.
With WS facing rejoin A to neck edge
of rem sts for right back and work as
given for left back from *** to end.

SLEEVES (make 2)

With 3¼mm (US 3) needles and MC,
cast on 48(52)sts and work in K2, P2,
rib for 6cm (2¼in).
Increase row: Rib 2(4), M1, [rib 2, M1,
rib 1, M1] 14 times, rib 2, M1, rib 2(4).
[78(82)sts.]
Change to 4mm (US 5) needles and
starting with a K row, work in st st, inc
1st at each end of every foll 5th row
until there are 122(126)sts on the
needle, thus ending with a WS row.
(Sleeve measures approx 42.5cm
(16¾in) from cast-on edge.)
Work 0(4) rows. Break off MC, join in
A.
Work 5 rows in A, place a marker at
each end of last row.
Cont straight in A and work a further
3.5(4.5)cm [1½(1¾)in] in st st.
Cast off all sts fairly loosely.

POLO COLLAR (worked separately)

With the 3¼mm (US 3) circular
needle and A, cast on 180sts and work
in **rounds** of K2, P2, rib for 10cm
(4in).
Change to the 4mm (US 5) circular
needle and cont in rib in rounds until
collar measures 20cm (7¾in) from
cast-on edge.
Break off A, join in MC.
*Next round: K.
Work 4 rounds in rib. *
Break off MC, join in A and work from
* to * once.
Cast off fairly loosely in rib in A.

NECKBAND

Join right shoulder seam.
With 3¼mm (US 3) needles and A,
pick up and K58(60)sts around front
neck and 46(48)sts around back neck.
[104(108)sts.]
Work in K2, P2, rib for 3cm (1¼in).
Cast off fairly loosely ribwise.

TO MAKE UP

Join left shoulder seam and neckband. With centre of cast-off edges of sleeves to shoulder seams, sew sleeves carefully in position joining seam above markers to cast-off sts at underarm. Join side and sleeve seams. Embroider eyes, using chain stitch and French knots, as shown.

WHITE PELICAN
Pelicanus onocrotalus

Laertes: To his good friends thus wide I'll ope my arms:
　　　　And like the kind life-rendering pelican
　　　　Repast them with my blood
　　　　　　　Hamlet IV v William Shakespeare

Pelicans were supposed to have fed their young with their own
blood and were represented in heraldry as 'a Pelican in her piety'
(piety in the classical sense of filial devotion), having pierced
their own breasts with their beaks.

In Christian art the Pelican is a symbol of charity and an
emblem of Jesus Christ, by 'whose blood we are healed'.
St Jerome says that the Pelican restored its chicks with the blood
of Christ when they were killed by serpents.

What else can I tell you about the Pelican? Well, I can tell you
that the Pelican State in America is Louisiana, that the Spanish and
Portuguese call them 'alcatraz' because these birds once lived on
the prison island in San Francisco Bay and it is true that its beak
can hold more than its belly can – nearly three gallons which
is two or three times its stomach capacity.

I spent some time in Los Angeles once, staying at a
friend's house on the beach at Malibu (devastatingly
glamorous!) and the most exciting thing of all
was watching the Pelicans fishing. They were
brown Pelicans, not the White variety and
I used to watch them for hours. I think it
was considered very eccentric behaviour,
to prefer watching these amazing birds to
going to some Hollywood party!

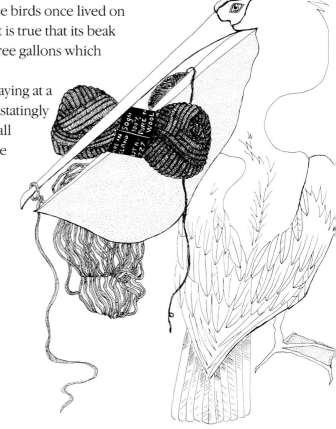

122

123

MEASUREMENTS

To fit bust: 81–86(91–97)cm
[32–34(36–38)in].
Actual measurement: 105(116)cm
[41¼(45¾)in].
Length from back neck: approx
61(63)cm [24(25)in].
Sleeve seam: 43(44)cm [17(17½)in].

MATERIALS

10(12) 50g balls of Sunbeam Sapphire
DK in turquoise (904) – MC.
1 ball in each of white (901) – A; pink
(911) – B; blue-grey (903) – C; black
(900) – D; yellow (909) – E.
1 pair each of 3¼mm (US 3) and 4mm
(US 5) needles.
Spare needle.
Stitch holder.

TENSION

22sts and 30 rows to 10cm (4in) using
4mm (US 5) needles and st st using
MC.

FRONT

With 3¼mm (US 3) needles and MC,
cast on 95(105)sts and work in single
rib as follows:
1st row: (RS facing) K1, *P1, K1, rep
from * to end.
2nd row: P1, *K1, P1, rep from * to
end.
Rep these 2 rows until rib measures
8cm (3¼in), ending with a first row.
Increase row: Rib 3, M1, [rib 5, M1, rib
4, M1] 10(11) times, rib 2(3).
[116(128)sts.]
Change to 4mm (US 5) needles and
starting with a K row, work 10 rows
straight in st st.
Joining in and breaking off colours as
required, cont in st st and colour patt
from chart, working between
appropriate lines for size required.
11th row: (RS facing) K88(94)MC,
K4A, K24(30)MC.
12th row: P21(27)MC, P10A,
P85(91)MC.
The chart is now placed.

Cont in patt from chart noting that the
central A panel is worked in reversed
st st, until 78 rows of st st in all have
been completed, thus ending with a
WS row.

Shape raglans

Keeping patt correct, cast off 3sts at
beg of next 2 rows.
3rd row: K2, K2tog tbl, patt to last 4sts,
K2tog, K2.
4th, 5th and 6th rows: Work in patt.
Rep 3rd to 6th rows 5(3) times more.
[98(114)sts.]
Now rep 3rd and 4th rows only until
56(58)sts rem, ending with a 4th row.

Shape front neck

Next row: (RS facing) K2, K2tog tbl,
K13 and leave these 16sts on a spare
needle for left front, cast off next
22(24)sts, K to last 4sts, K2tog, K2, and
cont on this last set of 16sts only for
right front.
Work 1 row.
** Still dec at raglan edge as before on
next row and then every foll alt row,
at the same time, dec 1st at neck edge
on next 8 rows, then on foll alt row.
[2sts.]
Next row: Work 2tog and fasten off.
With WS facing rejoin MC to neck
edge of rem sts for left front and work
1 row.
Now work as given for right front
from ** to end.

BACK

Work as given for front, omitting
colour patt and neck shaping, until
38(40)sts rem in raglan shaping,
ending with a WS row.
Leave sts on a stitch holder for back
neck.

LEFT SLEEVE

With 3¼mm (US 3) needles and MC,
cast on 45(47)sts and work in single
rib as given for front welt for 8cm
(3¼in), ending with a first row.

Increase row: Rib 3(1), M1, [rib 2, M1]
20(22) times, rib 2. [66(70)sts.]
Change to 4mm (US 5) needles, join
in A and K2 rows. Break A.
Now starting with a K row, cont in st st
in MC, inc 1st at each end of 5th row
and then every foll 4th row until there
are 106(112)sts on the needle.
Now work straight until sleeve
measures 43(44)cm [17(17½)in] from
cast-on edge, ending with a WS row.

Shape raglan

Cast off 3sts at beg of next 2 rows.
3rd row: K2, K2tog tbl, K to last 4sts,
K2tog, K2.
4th row: P.
Rep 3rd and 4th rows until 32sts rem,
ending with a 4th row. ***

Divide for top

Next row: (RS facing) K2, K2tog tbl,
K11, cast off next st and leave these
14sts on a spare needle for back
sleeve, K to last 4sts, K2tog, K2, and
cont on this last set of 15sts only for
front of sleeve.
Still dec at raglan edge as before on
foll 4 alt rows, **at the same time,** dec
1st at neck edge on next 9 rows. [2sts.]
Next row: Work 2tog and fasten off.
With WS facing rejoin MC to rem 14sts
for back sleeve, P2tog, P to end.
Still dec at raglan edge as before on
next row and foll 6 alt rows, **at the
same time,** dec 1st at neck edge on
every foll 3rd row 4 times. [2sts.]
Work 1 row.
Next row: Work 2tog and fasten off.

RIGHT SLEEVE

Work as given for left sleeve to ***

Divide for top

Next row: (RS facing) K2, K2tog tbl,
K12, cast off next st and leave these
15sts for front on a spare needle, K to
last 4sts, K2tog, K2.
Cont on rem 14sts for back sleeve and
still dec at raglan as before on foll 7 alt
rows, **at the same time,** dec 1st at neck

edge on next row and every foll 3rd row 4 times. [2sts.]
Work 1 row.
Next row: Work 2tog and fasten off.
With WS facing rejoin MC to rem 15sts for front sleeve, P2tog, P to end.
Still dec at raglan as before on next row and foll 3 alt rows, **at the same time**, dec 1st at neck edge on next 8 rows. [2sts.]
Next row: Work 2tog and fasten off.

NECKBAND
Join raglans, leaving left back raglan open.
With 3¼mm (US 3) needles and A and RS facing, pick up and K22sts along top of left sleeve, 44(46)sts around front neck, 22sts along top of right sleeve, then K across the 38(40)sts from back inc 1st at centre.
[127(131)sts.]
Next row: (WS facing) K. Break A, join in MC.
Next row: K.
Now starting with a 2nd row, work 5 rows in single rib as given for front welt.
Cast off fairly loosely ribwise.

TO MAKE UP
Join rem raglan and neckband seam.
Join side and sleeve seams.
Embroider eye, using chain stitch and a French knot, as shown.

RED JUNGLEFOWL

Gallus gallus

The ancestor of chicken mayonnaise,
Precursor of *le poulet hollandaise*,
Great-grandfather of *pâté de volaille*
And forebear of the great Kentucky fry,
Is the Junglefowl, a wild and wondrous bird,
Known in Asia long before we'd heard
Of scrambled eggs and other recipes.
This bird was praised by Aristophanes
And, long ago, the Romans took a shine
To *coq au vin* (or Junglefowl in wine)
And brought the bird to Britain when they came.
Since then it has enjoyed a certain fame.
Approximately three score fowl and ten
Make up the species of domestic hen
Descended from the Junglefowl. It's said
That nothing beats a plump Rhode Island Red –
But what about the Yokohama Cock,
The Silver Campine and the Plymouth Rock,
The Faverolle, Welsummer and Maran
La Bresse, Ancona, Red Cap and Houdan,
The Black Minorca or the Wyandotte
Or Chaucer's Chanticleer and Pertelote?
So when you have an egg on toast for tea
Just think about its noble ancestry;
'The chicken or the egg' dispute is hot
But the Junglefowl's the father of the lot.

MEASUREMENTS

To fit bust: 81–86(91–97)cm [32–34(36–38)in].

Actual measurement: 103(112)cm [40½(44)in].

Length from shoulder: approx 60(61)cm [23½(24)in].

Sleeve seam: 46(47)cm [18(18½)in].

MATERIALS

11(12) 50g balls of Phildar Sagittaire in pale grey (36) – MC.

1 ball in each of dark grey (43) – A; plum (42) – B; turquoise (95) – C; red (84) – D.

1 50g ball of Phildar Skate in yellow (12) – E.

3 20g balls of Phildar Sunset in gold (72) – F.

1 pair each of 3¼mm (US 3) and 3¾mm (US 4) needles.

3¼mm (US 3) circular needle.

Spare needle.

TENSION

22sts and 32 rows to 10cm (4in) using 3¾mm (US 4) needles over st st using MC.

NOTE

When using Phildar Sunset (F) use 3 strands together throughout.

FRONT

With 3¼mm (US 3) needles and MC, cast on 101(111)sts and work in single rib as follows:

1st row: (RS facing) K1, *P1, K1, rep from * to end.

2nd row: P1, *K1, P1, rep from * to end.

Rep these 2 rows until rib measures 8cm (3¼in), ending with a first row.

Increase row: Rib 6(8), M1 [rib 7(8), M1, rib 8, M1] 6 times, rib 5(7). [114(124)sts.]

Change to 3¾mm (US 4) needles and K1 row.

Joining in and breaking off colours as required, cont in st st and colour patt from chart, working between appropriate lines for size required.

2nd row: (WS facing) P65(70)MC, P1A, P48(53)MC.

3rd row: K49(54)MC, K1A, K64(69)MC.

The chart is now placed.

Cont in patt from chart until 85 rows of st st in all have been completed, thus ending with a RS row.

Divide for front neck

Next row: (WS facing) Patt 56(61), and leave these sts on a spare needle for right front, cast off 2sts, patt to end of row and cont on this last set of 56(61)sts only for left front.

** Keeping patt correct, dec 1st at neck edge on 5th row and then at this edge on every foll 4th row until 37(41)sts rem.

Work 3 rows, thus ending at side edge.

Shape shoulder

Cast off 9(10)sts at beg of next row and foll 2 alt rows, **at the same time**, dec once more at neck edge **for 2nd size only**.

Work 1 row.

Cast off rem 10sts.

With RS facing rejoin MC to neck edge of rem sts for right front and work as for left front from ** to end, but working 4 rows before shoulder shaping, thus ending at side edge.

BACK

Work as given for front, omitting colour patt and neck shaping, until back measures the same as front to beg of shoulder shaping, ending with a WS row.

Shape shoulder

Cast off 9(10)sts at beg of next row.

Next row: (WS facing) Cast off 9(10)sts, P until there are 40(44)sts on right-hand needle, and leave these sts on a spare needle for left back, cast off next 16sts, P to end of row and cont on this last set of 40(44)sts only for right back.

Cast off 9(10)sts at beg of next row.

Cast off 6(7)sts at beg (neck edge) of foll row.

Rep last 2 rows once more.

Cast off rem 10sts.

With RS facing rejoin MC to neck edge of rem sts for left back.

Cast off 6(7)sts at beg (neck edge) of next row.

Cast off 9(10)sts at beg of foll row.

Rep last 2 rows once more. Work 1 row.

Cast off rem 10sts.

SLEEVES (make 2)

With 3¼mm (US 3) needles and MC, cast on 53(57)sts and work in single rib as given for front welt for 5cm (2in), ending with a first row.

Increase row: Rib 3(1), M1, [rib 3, M1] 16(18) times, rib 2. [70(76)sts.]

Change to 3¾mm (US 4) needles and starting with a K row, work in st st, inc 1st at each end of 5th row and then every foll 6th row until there are 106(110)sts on the needle. Now inc 1st at each end of every foll 4th row until there are 112(120)sts on the needle.

Work straight until sleeve measures 46(47)cm [18(18½)in] from cast-on edge, ending with a WS row.

Cast off all sts fairly loosely.

NECKBAND

Join both shoulder seams.

With the 3¼mm (US 3) circular needle and MC and RS facing and starting at centre of V neck, pick up and K71(75)sts up right front neck, 45(49)sts across back neck and finally 71(75)sts down left front to V. [187(199)sts.]

Starting with a 2nd row, work in **rows** of single rib as given for front welt for 2cm (¾in), ending with a WS row.

Cast off fairly loosely ribwise.

129

TO MAKE UP
Place right side of neckband over left
side at centre front and join ends
neatly to pick-up row. Place a marker
at each side 25(27)cm [10(10½)in]
below shoulder seams. With centre of
cast-off edges of sleeves to shoulder
seams, sew sleeves in place between
markers. Join side and sleeve seams.
Embroider eyes, using chain stitch
and French knots, as shown.
Using back stitch work division of
beaks, and embroider legs and feet of
chick as shown.

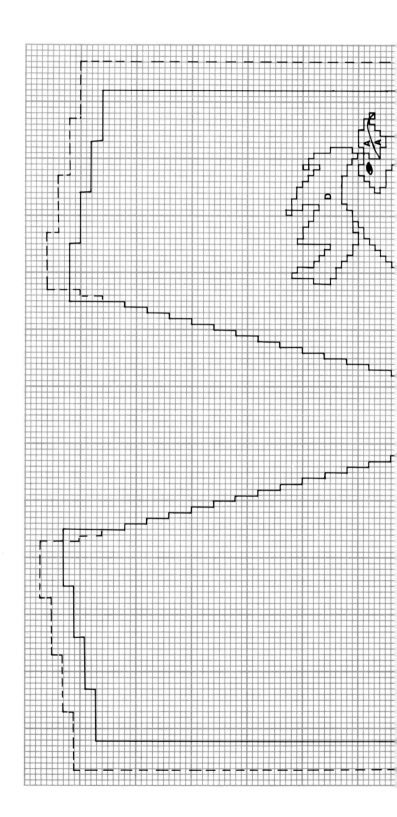

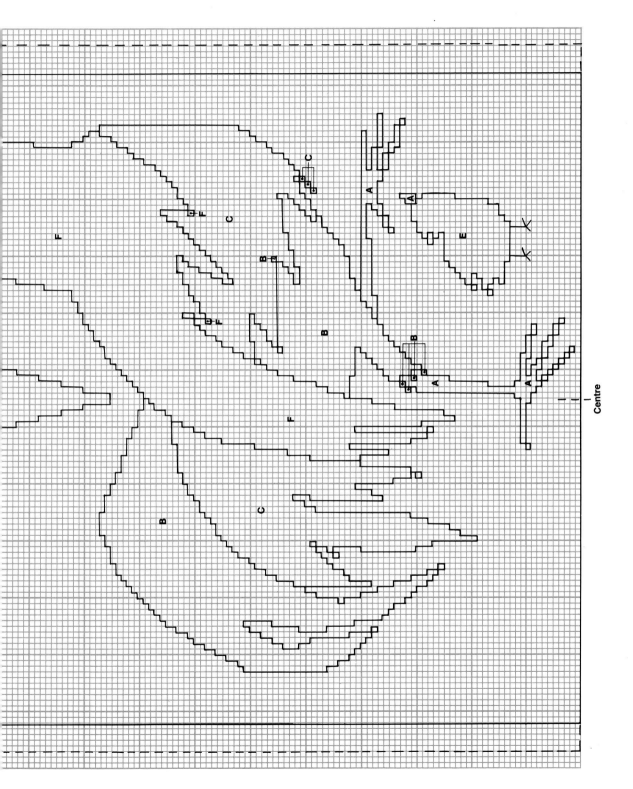

Centre

EMU

Dromiceius novae-hollandiae

The Emu is a ratite bird;
The ostrich is one, too.
This may not be a well-known word
So I'll explain to you

That ratite means, beneath its breast
It doesn't have a keel
And so, unlike the feathered rest,
It's had a rotten deal.

It cannot fly. A sorry state,
When facing enemies
The Emu doesn't sit and wait,
It turns its tail and flees.

At thirty miles an hour, it's fast
Although I wouldn't bet
That in a race it would outlast
The likes of Steve Ovett.

MEASUREMENTS

To fit bust: 81–86(91–97)cm [32–34(36–38)in].

Actual measurement: 107(117)cm [42(46)in].

Length from shoulder: approx 61(63)cm [24(24¾)in].

Sleeve seam: 43(44)cm [17(17½)in].

MATERIALS

11(13) 50g balls of Emu Superwash Chunky in royal blue (2713) – MC.

1 ball in grey (2775) – A.

1 50g ball of Emu Filigree in each of speckled grey (6373) – B; white (6378) – C; black (6370) – D; 2 balls in royal blue (6312) – E.

1 pair each of 4½mm (US 6) and 5½mm (US 8) needles.

Spare needle.

Crochet hook.

TENSION

16sts and 22 rows to 10cm (4in) using 5½mm (US 8) needles and st st using MC.

FRONT

With 4½mm (US 6) needles and MC, cast on 78(84)sts and work in K1, P1, rib for 8cm (3¼in).

Increase row: Rib 4(6), M1, [rib 10(8), M1] 7(9) times, rib 4(6). [86(94)sts.] **

Change to 5½mm (US 8) needles and starting with a K row, work 11 rows straight in st st.

Joining in and breaking off colours as required, cont in st st and colour patt from chart, working between appropriate lines for size required.

12th row: (WS facing) P50(54)MC, P3A, P1MC, P1A, P31(35)MC.

13th row: K30(34)MC, K1A, K1MC, K7A, K47(51)MC.

The chart is now placed.

Cont in patt from chart until 58 rows of st st in all have been completed, thus ending with a WS row.

Shape armholes

Keeping patt correct, cast off 3(4)sts at

beg of next 2 rows.

Dec 1st at each end of next 5 rows, then foll 1(2) alt row(s). [68(72)sts.]

Cont in patt from chart until 108(112) rows of st st in all have been completed, thus ending with a WS row.

Shape front neck

Next row: K25(26), and leave these sts on a spare needle for left front, cast off next 18(20)sts, K to end of row and cont on this last set of 25(26)sts only for right front.

Dec 1st at neck edge on next 7 rows. [18(19)sts.]

Work 1 row, thus ending at armhole edge.

Shape shoulder

Cast off 9(10)sts at beg of next row.

Work 1 row.

Cast off rem 9sts.

With WS facing rejoin MC to neck edge of rem sts for left front, P2 tog, P to end. [24(25)sts.]

Now dec 1st at neck edge on next 6 rows, [18(19)sts], thus ending at armhole edge. Shape shoulder as for right front.

BACK

Work as given for front to **.

Change to 5½mm (US 8) needles and starting with a K row, work 14 rows straight in st st.

Joining in and breaking off colours as required, cont in st st and colour patt from chart, working between appropriate lines for size required.

15th row: (RS facing) K54(58)MC, K1A, K31(35)MC.

16th row: P30(34)MC, P1A, P55(59)MC.

The chart is now placed.

Cont in patt from chart until chart is complete. Now cont in MC only, and work as given for front, omitting front chart and neck shaping, until 2 rows less than on front have been worked

to beg of shoulder shaping, ending with a WS row.

Shape back neck and shoulder

Next row: K23(25), and leave these sts on a spare needle for right back, cast off next 22sts, K to end of row and cont on this last set of 23(25)sts only for left back.

Work 1 row.

*** Cast off 5(6)sts at beg (neck edge) of next row, then 9(10)sts at beg of foll row.

Work 1 row.

Cast off rem 9sts.

With WS facing rejoin MC to neck edge of rem sts for right back and work as given for left back from *** to end.

SLEEVES (make 2)

With 4½mm (US 6) needles and MC, cast on 46(50)sts and work in K1, P1, rib for 8cm (3¼in).

Increase row: Rib 2(4), M1, [rib 6, M1] 7 times, rib 2(4). [54(58)sts.]

Change to 5½mm (US 8) needles and starting with a K row work in st st, inc 1st at each end of 5th row and then every foll 6th row until there are 64(66)sts on the needle. Now inc 1st at each end of every foll 4th row until there are 84(90)sts on the needle.

Work straight until sleeve measures 43(44)cm [17(17½)in] from cast-on edge, ending with a WS row.

Shape top

Cast off 3(4)sts at beg of next 6 rows, 4sts at beg of foll 4 rows, 5sts at beg of next 4 rows, then 6sts at beg of foll 2 rows.

Cast off rem 18sts fairly loosely.

COLLAR

With 4½mm (US 6) needles and E, cast on 69(73)sts and work in rib as follows:

1st row: (RS facing) K2, *P1, K1, rep from * to last st, K1.

2nd row: P2, *K1, P1, rep from * to last st, P1.

Rep these 2 rows once.

Keeping rib correct, shape by working turning rows as follows:

Next row: Rib to last 8sts, turn.

Next row: Sl 1, rib to last 8sts, turn.

Cont in this way, working 8sts fewer on next 4 rows.

Next row: Sl 1, rib to end.

Work 4 rows in rib across all sts using one 4½mm (US 6) needle and one 5½mm (US 8) needle.

Cont in rib using 5½mm (US 8) needles until collar measures 15cm (6in), measured up centre.

Cast off fairly loosely ribwise.

NECKBAND

Join right shoulder seam.

With 4½mm (US 6) needles and MC and RS facing, pick up and K44(46)sts evenly around front neck, then 36(38)sts evenly around back neck. [80(84)sts.]

Work in K1, P1, rib for 7 rows.

Cast off fairly loosely ribwise.

TO MAKE UP

Join left shoulder seam and neckband. Beg and ending at centre front, sew cast-on edge of collar into neck opening along WS of pick-up row. Fold collar over neck border so that K2 at each end lies to the front. Join side and sleeve seams. With centre of cast-off edges of sleeves to shoulder seams, sew sleeves carefully into armholes.

Embroider eyes, using chain stitch and French knots, as shown.

Cut remainder of B into 12cm (5in) lengths and using a crochet hook, loop under horizontal threads of emu to create a shaggy fringed effect.

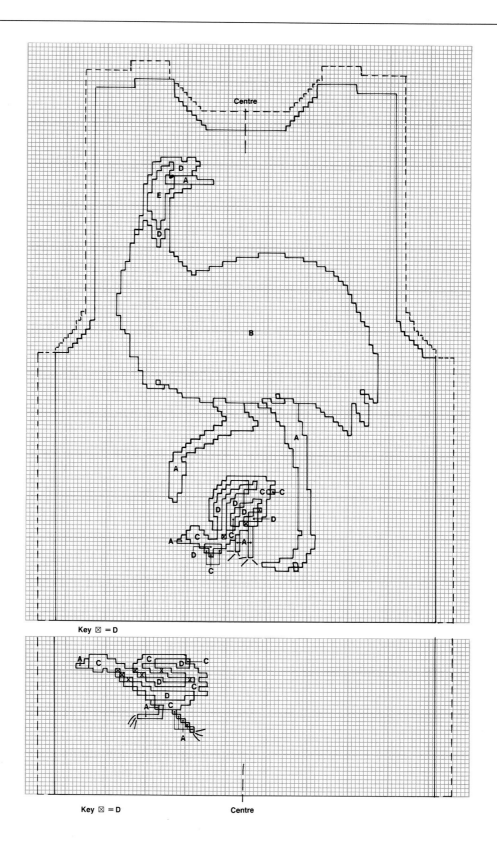

Key ⊠ = D

Key ⊠ = D   Centre

BLUE TITS
Parus caeruleus

On a tree by a river a little tom-tit
Sang 'Willow, titwillow, titwillow!'
And I said to him, 'Dicky-bird, why do you sit
Singing 'Willow, titwillow, titwillow?'
'Is it weakness of intellect birdie?' I cried,
'Or a rather tough worm in your little inside?'
With a shake of his poor little head he replied,
'Oh, willow, titwillow, titwillow!'

He slapp'd at his chest as he sat on that bough,
Singing 'Willow, titwillow, titwillow!'
And a cold perspiration be-spangled his brow,
Oh, willow, titwillow, titwillow!
He sobb'd and he sigh'd and a gurgle he gave,
Then he threw himself into a billowy wave,
And an echo arose from the suicide's grave,
'Oh, willow, titwillow, titwillow!'

Now I feel just as sure as I'm sure that my name
Isn't 'Willow, titwillow, titwillow!'
That 'twas blighted affection that made him exclaim,
'Oh, willow, titwillow, titwillow!'
And if you remain callous and obdurate, I
Shall perish as he did, and you will know why,
Though I probably shall not exclaim as I die,
'Oh, willow, titwillow, titwillow!'
        The Mikado Sir William Schwenck Gilbert

MEASUREMENTS

To fit bust: 81–86(91–97)cm [32–34(36–38)in].

Actual measurement: 105(116)cm [41¼(45¾)in].

Length from shoulder: approx 60(62)cm [23½(24½)in].

Sleeve seam: 46(47)cm [18(18½)in].

MATERIALS

11(12) 50g balls of Emu Superwash DK in pale green (3085) – MC.

1 ball in each of dark green (3020) – A; turquoise (3072) – B; black (3070) – C; white (3078) – D; yellow (3095) – E; brown (3050) – F.

1 50g ball of Emu Glimmer in red (3762) – G.

1 pair each of 3¼mm (US 3), 3¾mm (US 4) and 4mm (US 5) needles.

2 buttons.

Spare needle.

2 safety pins.

TENSION

22sts and 30 rows to 10cm (4in) using 4mm (US 5) needles and st st using MC.

SPECIAL ABBREVIATION FOR THIS PATTERN

X on chart = using G, work into next st thus: [K1, yfwd] 3 times, K1, making 7sts, turn, K7, turn, P7, turn, K7.

Next row: P7tog in G.

FRONT

With 3¼mm (US 3) needles and MC, cast on 101(111)sts and work in single rib as follows:

1st row: (RS facing) K1, *P1, K1, rep from * to end.

2nd row: P1, *K1, P1, rep from * to end.

Rep these 2 rows until rib measures 14cm (5½in), ending with a first row.

Increase row: Rib 5(4), M1, [rib 6, M1, rib 7, M1] 7(8) times, rib 5(3). [116(128)sts.]

Change to 4mm (US 5) needles and starting with a K row, work 43(49) rows straight in st st.

Joining in and breaking off colours as required, cont in st st and colour patt from chart, working between appropriate lines for size required.

Next row: (WS facing) P51(57)MC, P9A, P56(62)MC.

Next row: K53(59)MC, K15A, K48(54)MC.

The chart is now placed.

Cont in patt from chart noting how **X** should be worked, until 90(96) rows of st st in all have been completed, thus ending with a WS row.

Divide for front opening

Next row: Patt 55(61), turn and leave rem sts on a spare needle, and cont on this first set of sts only for left front.
**

Cont straight in patt until 125(131) rows of st st in all have been completed, thus ending at front edge.

Shape front neck

Cast off 5(7)sts at beg of next row.

Dec 1st at neck edge on next 9 rows, then on foll alt row. [40(44)sts.]

Work 1 row, thus ending at side edge.

Shape shoulder

Cast off 10(11)sts at beg of next row and foll 2 alt rows.

Work 1 row.

Cast off rem 10(11)sts.

With RS facing slip centre 6sts on to a safety-pin, rejoin MC to next st, K to end. [55(61)sts.]

Now work as for left front from ** to end, but work 126(132) rows of st st before front neck shaping.

BACK

Work as given for front, omitting colour patt and neck shaping, until back measures 1 row less than on front to beg of shoulder shaping, ending with a RS row.

Shape back neck and shoulder

Next row: P50(56), and leave these sts on a spare needle for left back, cast off

next 16sts, P to end of row and cont on this last set of 50(56)sts only for right back.

*** 1st row: Cast off 10(11)sts, work to end.

2nd row: Cast off 5(6)sts (neck edge), work to end.

Rep these 2 rows. [20(22)sts.]

Cast off 10(11)sts at beg of next row.

Work 1 row.

Cast off rem 10(11)sts.

With RS facing rejoin MC to neck edge of rem sts for left back K to end. Now work as for right back from *** to end.

SLEEVES (make 2)

With 3¼mm (US 3) needles and MC, cast on 55(59)sts and work in single rib as given for front welt for 8cm (3¼in), ending with a first row.

Increase row: Rib 3(6), M1, [rib 3, M1, rib 4(3), M1] 7(8) times, rib 3(5). [70(76)sts.]

Change to 4mm (US 5) needles and starting with a K row, work in st st, inc 1st at each end of 5th row and then every foll 6th row until there are 88(94)sts on the needle. Now inc 1st at each end of every foll 4th row until there are 112(118)sts on the needle.

Work straight until sleeve measures 46(47)cm [18(18½)in] from cast-on edge, ending with a WS row.

Cast off all sts fairly loosely.

BUTTON BAND

Join both shoulder seams.

With 3¼mm (US 3) needles and MC, cast on 9sts and work in rib as follows:

1st row: (RS facing) K2, *P1, K1, rep from * to last st, K1.

2nd row: K1, *P1, K1, rep from * to end.

Rep these 2 rows until band, when slightly stretched, fits up left front from base of opening to beg of neck shaping, ending with a RS row and sewing in position as you go. **

Next row: Cast off 4sts, leave rem 5sts on a safety pin. Break yarn.

BUTTONHOLE BAND

With RS facing, 3¼mm (US 3) needles and MC, K across the 6sts from base of opening, inc 3sts evenly across. [9sts.] Work as for button band to **, ending with a WS row, with the addition of 2 buttonholes, top one to come 1cm (½in) below top of band, second one spaced evenly between base of opening and top buttonhole.

Buttonhole row: (RS facing) Rib 3, cast off 2sts, rib to end.

Next row: Rib, casting on 2sts over cast-off sts on previous row.

COLLAR

With 3¼mm (US 3) needles and MC, work across 9sts of buttonhole band thus: cast off 4sts, rib 5, then pick up and K27(29)sts up right front neck, 45(47)sts across back, 27(29)sts down left front neck, then rib 5 from button band. [109(115)sts.]

Starting with a first row, work in single rib as given for button band for 3cm (1¼in).

Work 6 rows in rib using one 3¼mm (US 3) needle and one 3¾mm (US 4) needle.

Change to 3¾mm (US 4) needles and work a further 2cm (¾in) in rib.

Change to 4mm (US 5) needles and cont in rib until collar measures 11cm (4½in). Cast off fairly loosely ribwise.

TO MAKE UP

Sew cast-on edge of button band behind buttonhole band at base of opening.

Place a marker at each side 25(27)cm [10(10½)in] below shoulder seams. With centre of cast-off edges of sleeves to shoulder seams, sew sleeves carefully in position between markers. Join side and sleeve seams. Sew on buttons to correspond with buttonholes. Embroider eyes, using chain stitch and French knots, as shown. Using chain stitch, embroider feet.

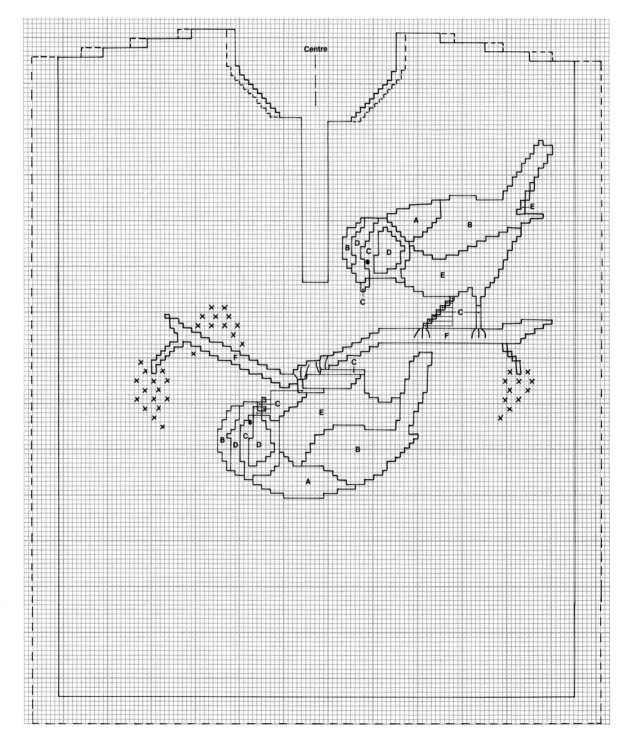

Centre

COMMON KINGFISHER
Alcedo atthis

My heart is like a singing bird
Whose nest is in a watered shoot;
My heart is like an apple-tree
Whose boughs are bent with thickset fruit;
My heart is like a rainbow shell
That paddles in a halcyon sea;
My heart is gladder than all these
Because my love is come to me.

from *A Birthday*
Christina Georgina Rossetti

Do you know why we refer to calm and peaceful times as 'halycon days'? I didn't, so just in case you don't, either, I'll tell you. The Greek word for Kingfisher is *halkyon* from *hals* (sea) and *kyon* (conceive). In Ovid's version of the legend of Ceyx and Alcyone, Ceyx is drowned in a shipwreck; the Gods take pity on his distraught wife, Alcyone, and turn them both into Kingfishers. Alcyone always nested at the edge of the sea and in the week before and the week after the winter solstice, Zeus calmed the waters so that Alcyone could hatch her chicks safely.

Another lovely Kingfisher legend describes how a dull, grey little bird flew from Noah's Ark after the flood, turned west into the setting sun where it scorched its breast a reddish gold and its wings and back turned blue from reflecting the sky.

MEASUREMENTS

To fit bust: 81–86(91–97)cm
[32–34(36–38)in].
Actual measurement: 103(113)cm
[40½(44½)in].
Length from shoulder: approx
58(60)cm [23(23½)in].

MATERIALS

11(13) 25g balls of Twilleys Lyscordet
No 5 in pale yellow (68) – MC.
1 ball in each of white (78) – A; black
(79) – B.
1 spool of Twilleys Gold Dust in each
of gold (2) – C; turquoise (37) – D;
purple (43) – E; red (38) – F.
1 pair each of 2¼mm (US 0) and
2¾mm (US 1) needles.
Spare needle.
2¼mm (US 0) circular needle.

TENSION

36sts and 44 rows to 10cm (4in) using
2¼mm (US 0) needles and st st using
MC.

NOTE

On chart, only motif is shown, and
sizes and shapings have been omitted,
due to the number of sts required.

FRONT

With 2¼mm (US 0) needles and MC,
cast on 155(171)sts and work in single
rib as follows:
1st row: (RS facing) K1, *P1, K1, rep
from * to end.
2nd row: P1, *K1, P1, rep from * to
end.
Rep these 2 rows until rib measures
8cm (3¼in), ending with a first row.
Increase row: Rib 2(6), M1, [rib 5, M1]
30(32) times, rib 3(5). [186(204)sts.]
Change to 2¾mm (US 1) needles and
starting with a K row work 35(43)
rows straight in st st. **
Joining in and breaking off colours as
required, cont in st st and colour patt
from chart.
Next row: (WS facing) P137(146)MC,
P1D, P48(57)MC.

Next row: K47(56)MC, K5D,
K134(143)MC.
The chart is now placed.
Cont in patt from chart until 202(210)
rows of st st in all have been
completed, thus ending with a WS
row.

Shape front neck

Next row: K76(83), and leave these sts
on a spare needle for left front, cast off
next 34(38)sts, K to end of row and
cont on this last set of 76(83)sts only
for right front.
Work 1 row.
*** Cast off 6sts at beg (neck edge) of
next row; then at same edge on foll alt
rows as follows: 5sts, 4sts, 3sts. Now
dec 1st at same edge on next 5 rows,
then on foll 2 alt rows. Cast off rem
51(58)sts.
With WS facing rejoin MC to rem sts
for left front and work as given for
right front from *** to end.

BACK

Work as given for front to **.
Cont straight in st st in MC only until
70 rows of st st in all have been
completed, thus ending with a WS
row.

Divide for V back

Next row: K89(98), K2tog, K2, turn
and leave rem sts on a spare needle
and cont on first set of 92(101)sts only
for right back.
Work 2 rows.
3rd row: P2, P2tog, P to end.
Work 2 rows.
6th row: K to last 4sts, K2tog, K2.
Rep last 6 rows until 72(81)sts rem.
Work 3 rows.
Next row: As 6th row.
Rep last 4 rows until 51(58)sts rem.
Now work a few rows straight until
back measures the same as front to
cast-off shoulder edge. Cast off all sts.
With RS facing rejoin MC to rem sts for

left back, K2, K2tog tbl, K to end of
row. [92(101)sts.]
Now work as for right back, reversing
shaping and working K2tog tbl in
place of K2tog.

BACK BORDER

Place a marker at each side of back
neck 2cm (¾in) below shoulders.
With the 2¼mm (US 0) circular
needle, and RS facing and MC, beg at
marker and pick up and K126(134)sts
down right side, 1st at point of V
(mark this st), then 126(134)sts up left
side to marker. [253(269)sts.]
1st row: (WS facing) *P1, K1, rep from
* to within 2sts of marked st, P2tog, P1,
P2tog tbl, ** K1, P1, rep from ** to end.
2nd row: K1, *P1, K1, rep from * to
within 2sts of marked st, P2tog, K1,
P2tog tbl, K1, ** K1, P1, rep from ** to
end.
Rep these 2 rows 3 times more.
Cast off loosely ribwise, dec as before.

NECKBAND

Join right shoulder seam.
With 2¼mm (US 0) needles and MC
and RS facing, pick up and
K96(100)sts evenly around front neck,
14sts down right back and across top
of back border, cast on 61(63)sts for
back neck, then pick up and K14sts
across top of back border and up left
back. [185(191)sts.]
Starting with a 2nd row work in single
rib as given for front welt for 8 rows.
Cast off fairly loosely ribwise.

TO MAKE UP

Join left shoulder seam and neckband.
Place a marker at each side of front
and back 28(30)cm [11(12)in] below
shoulder seams.

ARMHOLE BORDERS (alike)

With 2¼mm (US 0) needles and MC
and RS facing, pick up and
K181(195)sts between markers.
Starting with a 2nd row work in single

rib as given for front welt for 8 rows. Cast off fairly loosely ribwise.

TO COMPLETE
Join side seams and armhole borders.

Embroider eye, using chain stitch and a French knot, as shown.

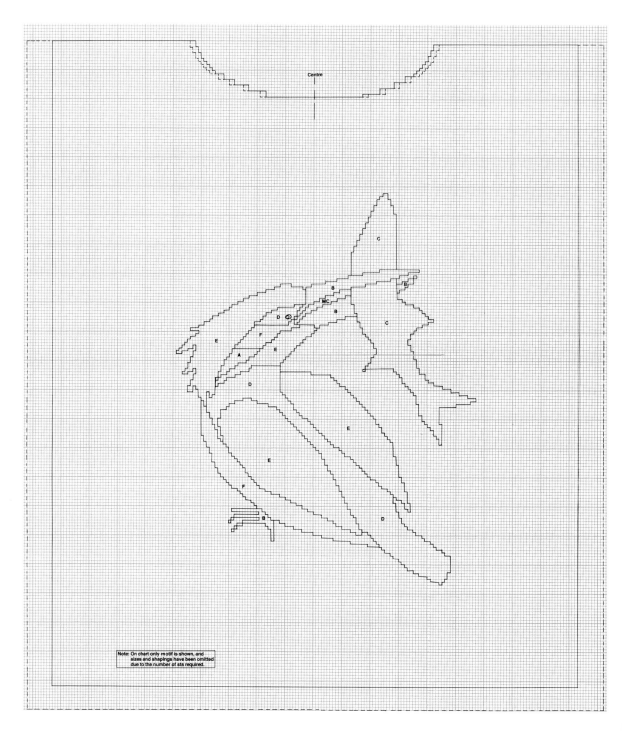

Centre

Note: On chart only motif is shown, and sizes and shapings have been omitted due to the number of sts required.

SCARLET MACAW
Ara macao

There once was a parrot who saw
It was better to sing than to caw
It little avail'd him
Creation had fail'd him
Which is why he's the Scarlet Macaw
                          Lord Birkett

There are over 300 kinds of parrot and their related species. They
come from all over the place – well, all over the tropical place
(what is known as pan-tropical) – the East Indies, Australia, New
Guinea, New Zealand, central Africa, the tropical rainforests of
Mexico, Central and South America and northwest India to
Thailand. Parrots, parakeets, Cockatoos, Cockateels, lories,
lorikeets, lovebirds, Macaws and Budgies are all in the same
group and they've got gorgeous names like the Kakapo, a rare
flightless parrot from New Zealand; the Kea, Spectacled parrotlet,
Eclectus parrot, Peach-faced lovebird, Hyacinth macaw, Crimson
Rosella, Rainbow lorikeet, Golden conure and the Military and
Scarlet Macaws.

Oliver Goldsmith has a good story in *Animated Nature* (1774):
A parrot belonging to King Henry VII, who then resided at
Westminster, in his palace by the river Thames, had learned to
talk many words from the passengers as they happened to
take the water. One day, sporting on its perch, the poor bird
fell into the water, at the same time crying out as loud as he
could 'A boat! Twenty pounds for a boat!' A waterman, who
happened to be near, hearing the cry, made to the place
where the parrot was floating, and taking him up, restored
him to the King. As it seems the bird was a favourite, the man
insisted that he ought to have a reward rather equal to his
services than his trouble: and as the parrot had cried twenty
pounds, he said the King was bound in honour to grant it. The
King at last agreed to leave it to the parrot's own
determination, which the bird hearing, cried out, 'Give the
knave a groat!'

MEASUREMENTS

To fit bust: 81–86(91–97)cm
[32–34(36–38)in].
Actual measurement: 106(117)cm
[41¾(46)in].
Length from shoulder: approx
59(61)cm [23¼(24)in].
Sleeve seam: 43(44)cm [17(17½)in].

MATERIALS

8(9) 50g balls of Hayfield Grampian
DK in black (024) – MC.
1 ball in each of silver birch (023) – E;
school grey (013) – F.
1 50g ball of Hayfield Hawaii DK in
each of red (029) – A; blue (030) – B;
yellow (043) – C; white (001) – D.
1 pair each of 3¼mm (US 3) and
4mm(US 5) needles.
Cable needle.
7 buttons.
1 crystal bead for eye.
2 spare needles.
2 safety pins.

TENSION

22sts and 28 rows to 10cm (4in) using
4mm (US 5) needles and st st using
MC.

SPECIAL ABBREVIATIONS FOR THIS PATTERN

C3L = slip next st on cable needle
and leave at front of work, K2, then K1
from cable needle.
C3R = slip next st on cable needle
and leave at back of work, K2, then K1
from cable needle.

PANEL PATTERN 1 (worked over 5sts)

1st row: (RS facing) P1, C3L, P1.
2nd row: K1, P3, K1.
These 2 rows form the **panel pattern 1**
and are repeated as required.

PANEL PATTERN 2 (worked over 5sts)

Work as for **panel pattern 1** working
C3R in place of C3L.

BACK

With 3¼mm (US 3) needles and MC,
cast on 102(110)sts and work in
double rib as follows:
1st row: (RS facing) K2, *P2, K2, rep
from * to end.
2nd row: P2, *K2, P2, rep from * to
end.
Rep these 2 rows until rib measures
5cm (2in), ending with a first row.
Increase row: Rib 7(3), M1, [rib 8(7),
M1] 11(15) times, rib 7(2).
[114(126)sts.]
Change to 4mm (US 5) needles and
starting with a K row, work 12 rows
straight in st st.
Joining in and breaking off colours as
required, cont in st st and colour patt
from chart, working between
appropriate lines for size required.
13th row: (RS facing) K78(84)MC,
K2A, K34(40)MC.
14th row: P34(40)MC, P2A,
P78(84)MC.
The chart is now placed.
Cont in patt from chart until 61 rows
of st st in all have been completed,
thus ending with a RS row.
Cont in colour patt, noting that 2nd,
3rd and 4th rows of perch (in E) are
worked in reversed st st.
65th row: K12(17)MC, M1 MC, patt to
last 12(17)sts, M1 MC, K12(17)MC.
[116(128)sts.]
66th row: P10(15)MC, **panel patt 2** as
2nd row in MC, patt to last 15(20)sts,
panel patt 1 as 2nd row in MC,
P10(15)MC.
67th row: K10(15)MC, **panel patt 1** as
first row in MC, patt to last 15(20)sts,
panel patt 2 as first row in MC,
K10(15)MC.
Cont in colour patt from chart and
panel patts as set until 78 rows of st st
in all have been completed, thus
ending with a WS row.

Shape armholes

Keeping patts correct, cast off 5(6)sts

at beg of next 2 rows. [106(116)sts.]
Cont straight in patts until 145(151)
rows of st st in all have been
completed.

Shape back neck

Next row: (WS facing) P 41(46) and
leave these sts on a spare needle for
left back, cast off next 24sts, P to end
of row and cont on this last set of
41(46) sts only for right back.
Work 1 row.
** Cast off 5(6)sts at beg (neck edge)
of next row and foll alt row.
Cast off rem 31(34)sts.
With RS facing rejoin MC to neck edge
of rem sts for left back and work as
given for right back from ** to end.

POCKET LININGS (make 2)

With 4mm (US 5) needles and MC,
cast on 29sts and starting with a K row
work straight in st st for 7cm (2¾in),
ending with a WS row.
Leave sts on a spare needle.

RIGHT FRONT

With 3¼mm (US 3) needles and MC,
cast on 60(64)sts and work in K2, P2,
rib for 4 rows.
Buttonhole row: (RS facing) Rib 4,
cast off 2sts, rib to end.
Next row: Rib, casting on 2sts over
cast-off sts on previous row.
Cont in rib as set until welt measures
5cm (2in), ending with a RS row.
Increase row: Rib 3(4), M1, rib 8(5),
M1, rib 5(6), M1, [rib 6(5), M1] 5(7)
times, rib 4, turn and slip rem 10sts on
to a safety-pin for buttonhole band.
[58(64)sts.]
Change to 4mm (US 5) needles and
cont in MC and patt as follows:
1st row: (RS facing) K43(44), **panel
patt 1** as first row, K10(15).
2nd row: P10(15), **panel patt 1** as 2nd
row, P43(44).
Rep these 2 rows until front measures
12cm (4¾in) from cast-on edge,
ending with a WS row.

Place pocket lining

Next row: K14(15), slip next 29sts on to a length of yarn and in place of them K across the 29sts from first pocket lining, **panel patt 1**, K10(15). Cont in patt across all sts until front measures the same as back to beg of armhole shaping, ending with a RS row.

Shape armhole

Cast off 5(6)sts at beg of next row. [53(58)sts.]
Now cont straight in patt until 15(17) rows less than on back have been worked to cast-off shoulder edge, ending at centre front edge.

Shape front neck

Cast off 10sts at beg of next row.
Work 1 row.
Cast off 4sts at beg of next row, then 3sts at beg of foll alt row.
Dec 1st at neck edge on next 3(5) rows, then on foll 2 alt rows.
Work 3 rows straight.
Cast off rem 31(34)sts.

LEFT FRONT

With 3¼mm (US 3) needles and MC, cast on 60(64)sts and work in P2, K2, rib until welt measures 5cm (2in), ending with a RS row.
Increase row: Rib 10 and slip these sts on to a safety-pin for button band, rib 4, M1, [rib 6(5), M1] 5(7) times, rib 5(6), M1, rib 8(5), M1, rib 3(4). [58(64)sts.]
Change to 4mm (US 5) needles and cont in MC and patt as follows:
1st row: (RS facing) K10(15), **panel patt 2** as first row, K43(44).
2nd row: P43(44), **panel patt 2** as 2nd row, P10(15).
Cont in patt as set and complete to match right front, reversing shapings and noting that place pocket lining row will read:
K10(15), **panel patt 2**, slip next 29sts on to a length of yarn and in place of

them K across the 29sts from 2nd pocket lining, K14(15).

SLEEVES (make 2)

With 3¼mm (US 3) needles and MC, cast on 48(52)sts and work in K2, P2, rib for 5cm (2in), ending with a RS row.

Increase row: Rib 1, M1, [rib 2, M1] 23(25) times, rib 1. [72(78)sts.]

Change to 4mm (US 5) needles and starting with a K row work in st st, inc 1st at each end of 5th row and then every foll 6th row until there are 78(82)sts on the needle. Now inc 1st at each end of every foll 4th row until there are 110(118)sts on the needle. Now work straight until sleeve measures 45(47)cm [17¾(18½)in] from cast-on edge, ending with a WS row.

Cast off fairly loosely.

POCKET BORDERS

Right front

With 3¼mm (US 3) needles and MC and RS facing, K across the 29sts from pocket top and inc 6sts evenly across. [35sts.]

Now work in rib as follows: ***

1st row: (WS facing) K1, P2, *K2, P2, rep from * to end.

2nd row: K2, *P2, K2, rep from * to last st, P1.

Rep these 2 rows until border measures 1.5cm (½in).

Cast off fairly loosely ribwise.

Left front

Work as for right front to ***.

1st row: (WS facing) P2, *K2, P2, rep from * to last st, K1.

2nd row: P1, K2, *P2, K2, rep from * to end.

Complete as for right front border.

BUTTON BAND

With 3¼mm (US 3) needles rejoin MC to the inside edge of 10sts at left front and work in rib as set until band, when slightly stretched, fits up left

front to start of neck shaping, ending with a WS row and sewing in place as you go.

Break yarn and leave sts on a safety-pin.

BUTTONHOLE BAND

Work as given for button band, with the addition of 6 buttonholes, last to come in centre of neckband, remainder spaced evenly between this and first buttonhole (already worked).

Buttonhole row: (RS facing) Rib 4, cast off 2sts, rib to end.

Next row: Rib, casting on 2sts over cast-off sts on previous row.

Do not break yarn on completion of buttonhole band.

NECKBAND

Join both shoulder seams.

With 3¼mm (US 3) needles and MC and RS facing, rib across the 10sts of buttonhole band, pick up and K26(28)sts up right front neck, 46(50)sts around back neck, 26(28)sts down left front neck and finally rib across the 10sts of button band. [118(126)sts.]

Starting with a 2nd row, work 3 rows in double rib as for back welt.

Make 7th buttonhole, as before, on next 2 rows.

Cont in rib until neckband measures 2cm (¾in).

Cast off fairly loosely ribwise.

TO MAKE UP

With centre of cast-off edges of sleeves to shoulder seams, sew sleeves carefully in position joining top of sleeve seam to cast-off sts at underarm.

Join side and sleeve seams. Join ends of pocket borders neatly to right side and slip stitch linings to wrong side of fronts. Sew on buttons to correspond with buttonholes. Embroider eye using chain stitch, and sew crystal bead in position, as shown.

151

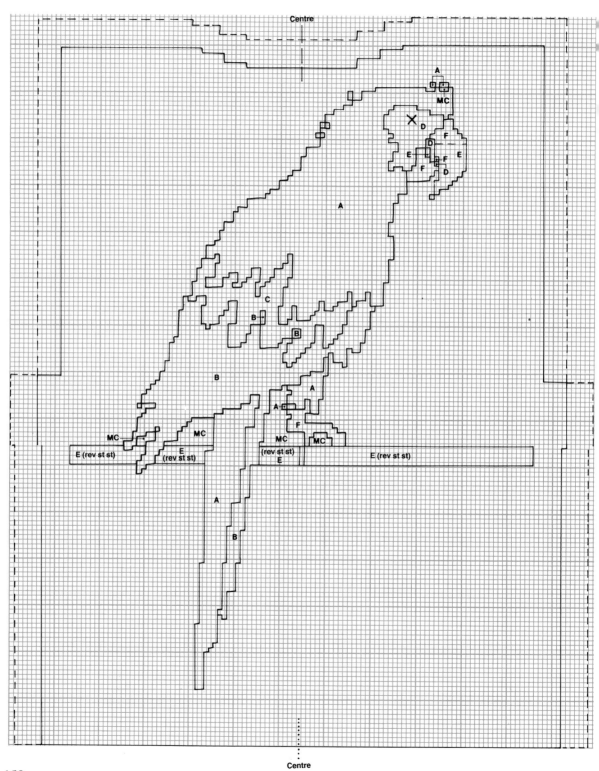

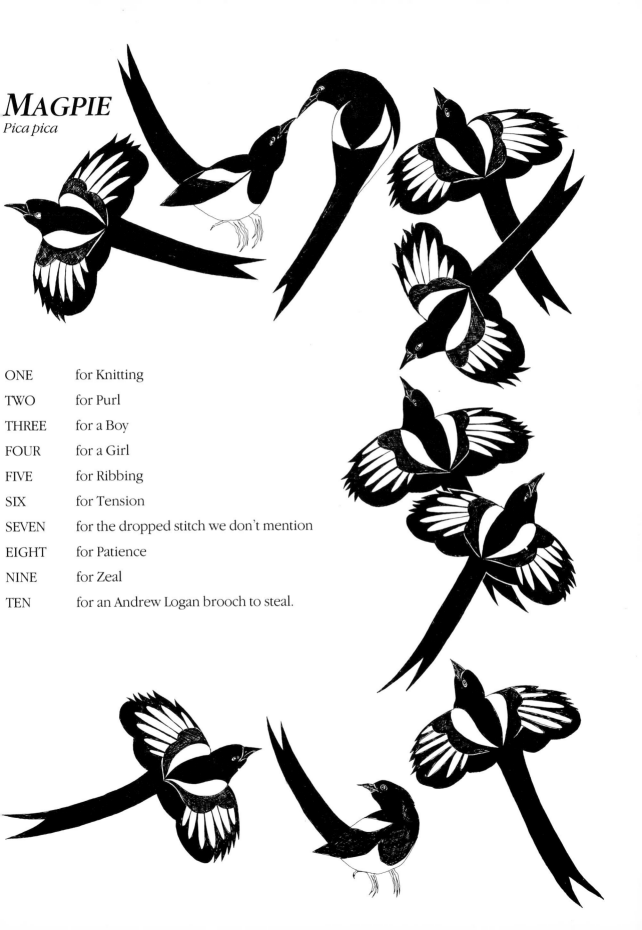

MAGPIE
Pica pica

ONE   for Knitting

TWO   for Purl

THREE   for a Boy

FOUR   for a Girl

FIVE   for Ribbing

SIX   for Tension

SEVEN   for the dropped stitch we don't mention

EIGHT   for Patience

NINE   for Zeal

TEN   for an Andrew Logan brooch to steal.

MEASUREMENTS

To fit bust: 81–86(91–97)cm
[32–34(36–38)in].
Actual measurement: 103(113)cm
[40½(44½)in].
Length from shoulder: approx
60(62)cm [23½(24½)in].
Sleeve seam: 33(34)cm [13(13½)in].

MATERIALS

10(11) 50g balls of Georges Picaud
Fascination in blue (22) – MC.
1 50g ball of Georges Picaud No 1 in
each of dark green (182) – A; navy
(87) – B; black (13) – C; white (1) – D.
1 20g ball of Georges Picaud Feu
D'Artifice in each of dark silver (30) –
E; steel blue (56) – F; silver (4) – G.
1 pair each of 3¾mm (US 4) and
4½mm (US 6) needles.
3¾mm (US 4) circular needle.
Spare needle.
Crystal button for eye.

TENSION

20sts and 34 rows to 10cm (4in) using
4½mm (US 6) needles and moss
stitch patt using MC.

NOTE

Georges Picaud No 1 and Georges
Picaud Feu D'Artifice yarns are to be
used **together** as follows:
Yarn A is to be used together with
yarn E.
Yarn B is to be used together with
yarn F.
Yarns C and D are to be used together
with yarn G.
The bird is knitted entirely in garter st,
but when changing from MC to
contrast, or from one contrast to
another, work **first** row K on RS and P
on WS.

FRONT

With 3¾mm (US 4) needles and MC,
cast on 91(101)sts and work in single
rib as follows:
1st row: (RS facing) K1, *P1, K1, rep
from * to end.

2nd row: P1, *K1, P1, rep from * to
end.
Rep these 2 rows until rib measures
10cm (4in), ending with a first
row.
Increase row: Rib 2(7), M1, [rib 8, M1]
11 times, rib 1(6). [103(113)sts.]
Change to 4½mm (US 6) needles and
moss stitch patt as follows:
1st row: K1, *P1, K1, rep from * to
end.
This row forms the moss stitch patt
and is repeated as required.
Rep this row 6 times more.
Joining in and breaking off colours as
required, cont in moss st and colour
patt from chart, working between
appropriate lines for size required.
8th row: (WS facing) Patt 89(94)MC,
P1A + E, patt 13(18)MC.
9th row: Patt 14(19)MC, K1A + E, patt
88(93)MC.
The chart is now placed.
Cont in patt from chart working bird
in garter st (see Note) until 162(168)
rows of patt in all have been
completed, thus ending with a WS
row.

Shape front neck

Next row: Patt 45(49), and leave these
sts on a spare needle for left front, cast
off next 13(15)sts, patt to end of row
and cont on this last set of 45(49)sts
only for right front.
Work 1 row.
** Cast off 3sts at beg (neck edge) of
next row and foll 3 alt rows.
Cast off rem 33(37)sts.
With WS facing rejoin MC to neck
edge of rem sts for left front and work
as given for right front from ** to end.

BACK

Work as given for front, working in
moss stitch patt and omitting colour
patt, until back measures 42(44)cm
[16½(17¼)in] from cast-on edge,
ending with a WS row.

Shape back neck

Next row: Patt 48(53), and leave these
sts on a spare needle for right back,
cast off next 7sts, patt to end of row
and cont on this last set of 48(53)sts
only for left back.
*** Dec 1st at neck edge on next 4
rows, then on foll 5 alt rows.
[39(44)sts.]
Work 3 rows.
Now dec 1st at neck edge on next row
and every foll 4th row until 33(37)sts
rem.
Now work straight in patt until back
measures the same as front to cast-off
shoulder edge.
Cast off.
With WS facing rejoin MC to neck
edge of rem sts for right back and
work as given for left back from *** to
end.

SLEEVES (make 2)

With 3¾mm (US 4) needles and MC,
cast on 59(63)sts and work in single
rib as given for front welt for 3cm
(1¼in), ending with a first row.
Increase row: Rib 3(5), M1, [rib 6, M1]
9 times, rib 2(4). [69(73)sts.]
Change to 4½mm (US 6) needles and
work in moss stitch patt as given for
front, **at the same time**, inc 1st at each
end of 7th row and then every foll 6th
row until there are 99(105)sts on the
needle, working inc sts into the patt.
Cont straight in patt until sleeve
measures 33(34)cm [13(13½)in] from
cast-on edge, ending with a WS row.
Cast off fairly loosely in patt.

NECKBAND

Join right shoulder seam.
With the 3¾mm (US 4) circular
needle and RS facing and MC, pick up
and K19sts down left front, 14(16)sts
across centre, 19sts up right front,
67(71)sts down right back, 5sts across
centre, then 67(71)sts up left back.
[191(201)sts.]
Starting with a 2nd row, work in

155

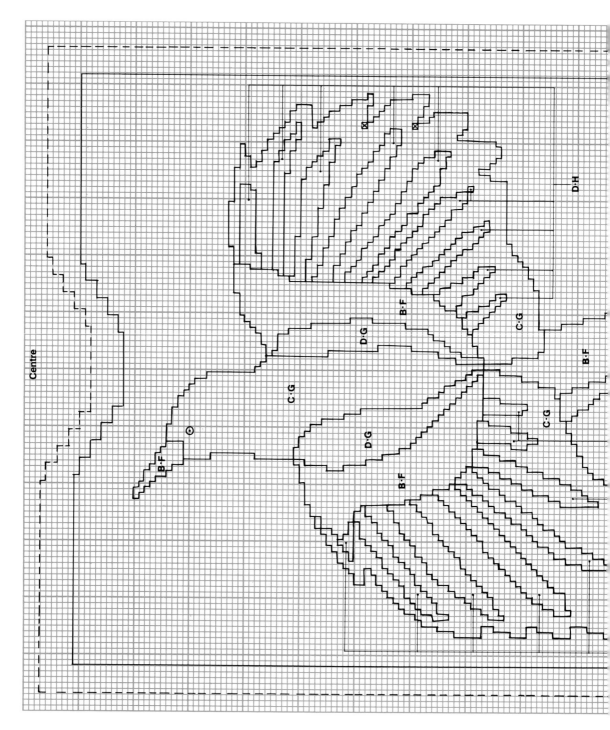

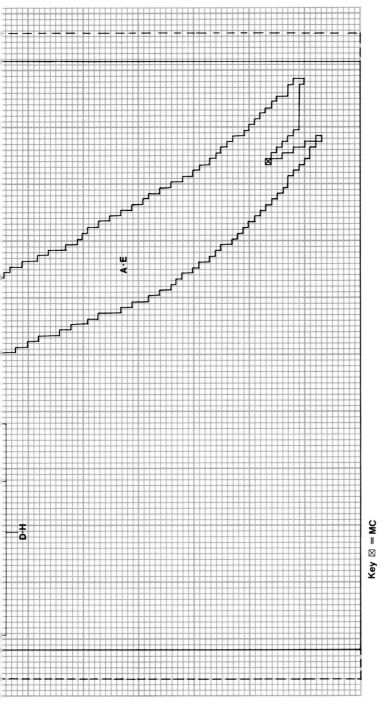

Key ⊠ = MC

single rib in **rows** as given for front welt for 4cm (1¾in).
Cast off fairly loosely ribwise.

TO MAKE UP

Join left shoulder seam and neckband. Fold neckband in half to inside and slip stitch loosely in position. Place a marker at each side of front and back 24(26)cm [9½(10¼)in] below shoulder seams. With centre of cast-off edges of sleeves to shoulder seams, sew sleeves in position between markers. Join side and sleeve seams. Sew crystal button in place, then embroider round eye, using chain stitch as shown.

LIST OF SUPPLIERS

The firms listed below are the suppliers of the yarns used in this book.

AVOCET
Avocet Hand Knitting Yarns
Hammerain House
Hookstone Avenue
Harrogate
Yorkshire HG2 8ER

Mail Order Stockist:
Bedford Wool Shop
The Old Arcade
Bedford

USA and Canada Agent:
Estelle Design & Sales Ltd
38 Continental Place
Scarborough, Ontario
Canada M1R 2T4

EMU
Emu Wools Ltd
Leeds Road
Greengates
Bradford
West Yorkshire BD10 9TE

Mail Order Stockist:
Ries Wools
242–243 High Holborn
London WC1V 7DZ

USA Agent:
The Plymouth Yarn Co Inc
PO Box 28
500 Lafayette Street
Bristol PA 19007
USA

HAYFIELD
Hayfield Textiles Ltd
Glusburn
Keighley
West Yorkshire BD20 8QP

Mail Order Stockist:
Best Wool Shop
26–28 Frenchgate
Doncaster
Yorkshire DN1 1QQ
or Bedford Wool Shop
The Old Arcade
Bedford

USA Agent:
Shepherd Wools Inc
711 Johnson Avenue
Blaine
Washington 98230
USA

PATONS
Patons & Baldwins Ltd
Alloa
Clackmannanshire
Scotland FK10 1EG

Mail Order Stockist:
Ries Wools
242–243 High Holborn
London WC1V 7DZ

USA Agent:
Susan Bates Inc
212 Middlesex Avenue
Route 9A, Chester
Connecticut 06412
USA

PHILDAR
Phildar UK Ltd
4 Gambrel Road
Westgate Industrial Estate
Northampton NN5 5NF

Mail Order Stockist:
Ries Wools
242–243 High Holborn
London WC1V 7DZ

USA Agent:
Phildar Inc
6438 Dawson Boulevard
85 North, Norcross
Georgia 30093
USA

PINGOUIN
Pingouin Corporation
7–11 Lexington Street
London W1R 4BU

Mail Order Stockist:
Write to the Lexington Street
address for the Pingouin stockist
nearest you

USA Agent:
PO Box 100
Highway 45
Jamestown
South Carolina SC29453
USA

PRIORY/GEORGES PICAUD
Priory Yarns Ltd
24 Prospect Road
Ossett
West Yorkshire WF5 8AE

Mail Order Stockist:
Write to the Ossett address for
the stockist nearest you

USA Agent:
230 Fifth Avenue
Suite 2000
New York 10001
USA

Georges Picaud
Usine de Mont d'Origny
02 Origny Ste Benoite
France

ROBIN
Robin Wool Ltd
Robin Mills
Idle
Bradford
West Yorkshire BD10 9TE

Mail Order Stockist:
Write to the West Yorkshire
address for the Robin Wool
stockist nearest you

USA Agent:
The Plymouth Yarn Co Inc
PO Box 28
500 Lafayette Street
Bristol PA 19007
USA

SCHEEPJESWOL
Scheepjeswol (UK) Ltd
PO Box 48
7 Colemeadow Road
Redditch
Worcestershire B98 9NZ

Mail Order Stockist:
Wyvern Yarns Ltd
2 Tuer Way
Inkberrow
Worcestershire WR7 4EQ

USA Agent:
Neveda Yarn Company Inc
8, 13th Avenue
Ronkonkoma
NY 117799
USA

SIRDAR
Sirdar PLC
Flanshaw Lane
Alverthorpe
Wakefield
West Yorkshire W12 9ND

Mail Order Stockist:
Best Wool Shop
26–28 Frenchgate
Doncaster
Yorkshire DN1 1QQ

USA Agent:
Kandex Corporation
10 Box 1909, 616 Sitch Avenue
Moorpark
California 93021
USA

SUNBEAM
Sunbeam Ltd
Crawshaw Mills
Pudsey
West Yorkshire LS28 7BS

Mail Order Stockist:
Write to the West Yorkshire
address for the Sunbeam stockist
nearest you

3 – SUISSES
3–Suisses
9 King Street
Leicester LE1 6RN

Mail Order Stockist:
3–Suisses
Rugby
Warwickshire

USA Agent:
Dominique Corporation
Empire State Building
Suite 2709, 350 Fifth Avenue
NY 10118
USA

TOTAL CRAFT
Total Craft Ltd
56 Oxford Street
Manchester M60 1HJ

Mail Order Stockist:
Ries Wools
242–243 High Holborn
London WC1V 7DZ

TWILLEYS
H G Twilley Ltd
Roman Mill
Stamford
Lincolnshire PE9 1BG

Mail Order Stockist:
Jay Craft
78 St Johns Street
Bury St Edmunds
Suffolk IP33 1SQ

USA Agent:
Rainbow Gallery Inc
13615 Victory Boulevard
Suite 245, Van Nuys
CA 91401
USA

WENDY
Wendy Wools
Carter & Parker
Gordon Mills
Guiseley
West Yorkshire LS20 9PD

Mail Order Stockist:
Ries Wools
242–243 High Holborn
London WC1V 7DZ

USA & Canada Agent:
White Buffalo Mills
545 Assiniboine Avenue
Brandon
Manitoba RGA 0G3
Canada